BLIND SPOT

"Deacon Charlie is not only a gifted communicator and incredible pastor; he is someone who walks the walk with God in an age when a lot of people just talk. Everyone should listen to what he has to say."

Ryan Bethea
Creator and cohost of *The Exorcist Files* podcast

"Like the Blessed Mother whom they so cherish, Latinos in America are the often-overlooked heart of the Church, humbly waiting for the call to do God's will. The Latino tree will bear much fruit, if only we have the wisdom to water it."

Julio Quintana
Director of *The Long Game*, *Blue Miracle*, and *The Vessel*

"Drawing on decades of experience, Deacon Charlie Echeverry shows how Latinos are poised to spark renewal of the Catholic Church in America and why that matters for everyone engaged in ministry today."

John Cannon
Founder of SENT Ventures

"Deacon Charlie Echeverry offers the Church a timely and compelling vision. With both pastoral wisdom and business acumen, he shows why Latinos are not only the heart of the Church in the United States but also its greatest hope for renewal. This book will energize anyone who longs to see the Church in America revived."

Jason Shanks
President of the National Eucharistic Congress

"Drawing from a data-informed approach and a wealth of experience, *Blind Spot* is delivering a timely and galvanizing message on how Latino Catholics are being called to the forefront of the revival God is bringing to his Church today. All leaders should be reading this book!"

Tim Glemkowski
Executive director of Amazing Parish

"As we anticipate and prepare for the five-hundredth anniversary of the apparitions of Our Lady of Guadalupe, this book could not be more timely or urgent. Deacon Charlie Echeverry offers a compelling and hope-filled vision that reminds us that the Latino experience is one of the most consequential realities in the Church today. This is a must read for anyone who cares about the future of Catholic life in America."

Vicente Del Real
Founder and executive director of Iskali

"Deacon Charlie Echeverry shows us that unleashing the Latino Catholic community's potential isn't optional. It is essential for evangelizing and revitalizing our postpandemic parishes. A must read for every Catholic leader ready to ignite the Church in America!"

Fr. Agustino Torres, CFR
Founder of Corazón Puro and author of *Prepare Your Heart* and *Made for Heaven*

"Religious transformation swept the Americas when Our Lady of Guadalupe appeared to Juan Diego. Deacon Charlie Echeverry points to her vision offering the Latino charism, which can reinvigorate the spiritual landscape of the Catholic Church in the United States. Her vision was clear; as Deacon Charlie points out, the blind spot becomes the pathway."

Berni Neal
Cofounder of the RBN Foundation

"I have long believed that the Church needs to raise up a new generation of strong Latino leaders, whose rich heritage of faith, family, and culture has the promise to renew our parishes, communities, and country. Deacon Echeverry believes that, too, and he shows us how we can make that happen. I encourage everyone to read this challenging and exciting book."

Archbishop José H. Gomez
Archdiocese of Los Angeles

"This book is both a wake-up call and a source of hope. Deacon Charlie Echeverry shows how the vitality of the Latino community can reignite the Church's missionary spirit across the nation and beyond."

Montse Alvarado
President and COO of EWTN News

BLIND

The Evangelizing Power of Latino Culture

SPOT

Deacon Charlie Echeverry

Ave Maria Press AVE Notre Dame, Indiana

Nihil Obstat: Reverend Monsignor Michael Heintz, PhD
Censor librorum

Imprimatur: Most Reverend Kevin C. Rhoades
Bishop of Fort Wayne–South Bend
Given at Fort Wayne, Indiana, on October 27, 2025

Founded in 1865, Ave Maria Press is a ministry of the United States Province of Holy Cross.

www.avemariapress.com

Paperback: ISBN-13 978-1-64680-433-7

E-book: ISBN-13 978-1-64680-434-4

Cover images © Getty Images and Unsplash.

Cover and text design by Andy Wagoner.

Printed and bound in the United States of America.

Library of Congress Cataloging-in-Publication Data is available.

To my parents,

OSCAR (†) AND HILDAMARIE ECHEVERRY,

who introduced me to my culture and, more importantly, to Christ.

CONTENTS

Part 1

1. Living in the Hyphen 3

2. Spiritual Heirs of St. Juan Diego 13

3. Our Flock 21

4. DEI and All That 35

5. What Makes Latinos Different? 39

6. The Power of Insights 43

Part 2: Insights

Insight 1: Go *Through* Latinos, Not Just *to* Latinos 51

Insight 2: Language Is a Tool; Culture Is a Gateway 57

Insight 3: Cultural Duality Is a Superpower 65

Insight 4: Cultural Catholicism Can Hamper Genuine Faith 71

Insight 5: Talent > Time > Treasure 81

Insight 6: Communion Surpasses Community 89

Insight 7: Don't Stress Differences; Build on Commonalities 99

A Challenge for My Latino Sisters and Brothers 105

Epilogue: What Next? 109

Notes 111

Illustration Credits 113

PART I

1
LIVING IN THE HYPHEN

I was born to an immigrant couple from Colombia in *Nuestra Señora, la Reina de Los Angeles*. Tinseltown. La-La Land. Los Angeles in common parlance. A place known by many appellations, but whose actual name does not describe a topographical feature or proceed from some rich benefactor's surname but instead signifies a *person*: Mary, the Mother of Jesus. The Mother of God. Our Lady, Queen of the Angels. Los Angeles, California.

My father, who for a few weeks experienced homelessness when he first arrived in the United States by way of Miami, eventually made it across the country to settle in the great sprawling metropolis of LA (first staying briefly in New York and in so doing completing the obligatory trifecta of Latino* immigrant geographic stops). Once settled he landed a job in the mailroom of an international bank while attending LA City College to gain his accreditations. He would go on to work at that same bank for nearly thirty years.

* Latino or Hispanic? The shorthand: **Hispanic = language** and **Latino = culture**. In this book, I use "Latino" almost exclusively. "Hispanic" refers to the term *de habla Hispana*, "of the Spanish tongue," so "Hispanic" refers principally to a **language** and the people who speak it. "Latino" refers principally to a **people**: the communities and cultures that either live in or have come from Mexico or elsewhere in Latin America, including parts of the Caribbean. These peoples mostly speak Spanish, but not exclusively. So, there are Hispanics who are not Latinos (think Spaniards or Andorrans) and Latinos who are not Hispanics (think Brazilians or Belizeans).

Dad hailed originally from the small town of Anserma, the oldest town in the department of Caldas: the world-famous coffee-growing region of Colombia.* He was one of five children born to a decidedly bohemian couple who had a penchant for the arts, international music, and ecological pursuits and who tended to leftist politics while by all accounts regarding their own inherited Catholicism as largely a cultural artifact.

My mother, on the other hand, was cut from a completely different cloth. She was the eldest girl in a family of thirteen born in Cali, the most populous city in the southwest of the country. Her father was a prominent banker and member of the new-world aristocracy that took root in Colombia between the Second World War and the Korean War. Her mother was a doting homemaker. Together, my maternal grandparents, despite the baker's dozen mouths to feed, provided their large family with the education, etiquette, and niceties of Colombia's polite society while managing to live a devout, albeit folkloric, Catholic faith.

Dad and Mom were rather a strange match to be sure, but God has his ways.

My father departed for the United States in 1961, leaving my mother behind in Colombia with a promise that once he'd settled in the country and saved some money, he'd return for her. Three cities, hundreds of letters, and multiple years later, he kept his word; he returned to Colombia, married my mother, and brought her back to the States to a small house in Downey, California, which was at that time a predominantly white, middle-class neighborhood in Los Angeles beginning to experience

* That's Colombia with an *o*, folks, not a *u*! No doubt among the most misspelled country names in the world, "Colombia" and the slightly older "Columbia" are both derived from "Cristoforo Colombo," the name of the famous Italian explorer we know as Christopher Columbus. Both refer to the same person, but few things are more irksome to Colombians than to see their country mislabeled with that anglicized *u*.

Dad and Mom at the dance where they first met, March 1960

rapid growth in its Latino population. After a few years, my brother and I were brought into the world: **first-generation Americans**.

Like most children, my brother and I were *formally* named by our parents, but family lore has it that we were given our much more important nicknames by our next-door neighbors: Art and Lilian Reed. They were a lovely, corpulent couple that embodied what I would later understand to be a Southern California version of mid-twentieth-century Americana.

My brother, the firstborn, was given the obligatory Hispanic double name by our parents—a nearly canonical requirement in Latino kid-name orthodoxy. He was to be called "Oscar Francisco." "Oscar" in honor of my dad, and "Francisco" ostensibly after St. Francis, although there were a number of "Franciscos" in the family who also may have served as provenance.

I, on the other hand, in an episode of cultural disobedience (or rebellion perhaps) on the part of my parents—an episode that was never fully explained despite many earnest inquiries—was given the otherwise unthinkable **single name**: the lonely and rather pedestrian "Carlos."

In turn, and almost immediately, Art and Lilian, flummoxed by the notion of having to pronounce the elegant but foreign-sounding "Oscar Francisco," or the brief yet equally ethnic "Carlos," opted instead to unilaterally declare us "Frankie" and "Charlie," illustrating in the process one of the hallmarks of the

American exceptionalism I'd eventually discover. That is our culture's remarkable ability to **brand** something, especially by employing a combination of ingenuity and brevity.

And crazy thing: The names stuck. So much so that my dad and mom—and even our extended family in Colombia (who we'd visit on summer breaks)—called us strictly by our American names. Frankie and Charlie. I don't exaggerate when I say that I cannot recall ever being called "Carlos" by anyone who wasn't wearing a badge or medical scrubs or was otherwise attempting to confirm my identity from a legal document.

My father, true to the old-school immigrant work ethic, was industrious and tireless. He labored in the cavernous mailroom of the bank until his talents were discovered, and he was eventually rewarded by securing an operations position supporting the Latin American and Caribbean division of the company.

In time, his know-how, personality, and multiple language skills made him a natural choice for one of the company's near-shore executive opportunities in Mexico. After some prayer and discernment, with two very young kids in tow, my father and mother, having only recently immigrated to the United States from Colombia, now emigrated from Los Angeles to Mexico City.

We stayed in Mexico for a few years. My brother and I attended British American School in Naucalpan, the preferred choice of the American expats in my dad's new professional circle. Mexico represented my formative childhood experience, my key developmental period: a strange blend of British headmasters, embossed blue blazers, and Anglo-Saxon teachers, coupled with the color, clamor, and folklore of kaleidoscopic Mexican culture that yielded in me a child one part Anglophile* and one part Chilango.†

It was, ironically, in Mexico, a country known for its Spanish and more than sixty indigenous dialects, where my brother and I first mastered the English language.

I hated English with a passion at first. I had no desire to learn it. It had a deep grammatical and phonetic illogic that made it impossible to anticipate (*two*, *too*, *to* . . . *bomb*, *tomb*, *comb*) and suffered from a lack of melody in its timbre that made me suspicious. English was nothing like the lovely romance language that I'd learned on my mother's lap and on adventures with my father.

Despite my misgivings about the language, years later, my brother and I would come to speak to each other *only* in English, while at the same time communicating with our parents exclusively (and zealously) in Spanish. This is a very common practice of bicultural kids even to this day. To speak to my parents in a language other than Spanish felt bizarre. I once described it to a friend as something akin to kissing your sister. Just weird.

When my parents didn't want us to know what they were saying, which was often, given our curiosity and general precociousness, they'd employ a pig-Latin variant of Spanish they called *Jerigonza*.‡ Years on, Frankie and I would eventually crack the code and learn to decipher that language too. We came to be quite adept at it, in fact. Yet for the better part of our elementary-school

* Only in my forties, and thanks to my wife, did I come to realize that the reason I like British television, ride British motorcycles, and occasionally observe teatime at 11 a.m. and 4 p.m. may have something to do with the British influence during key neurobiological years!

† Slang term for those from Mexico's capital, Mexico City. In context, it also tends to connote something akin to a **city slicker**: overconfident at best, elitist at worst.

‡ Pronounced "Hare-ee-gone-zah," this is a Spanish-language game played by kids in Spain and throughout Latin America. It originates from the Portuguese word *geringonça*, which oddly means "a complicated mechanical contraption." The game consists of adding the letter *p* after each vowel of a word and then repeating the vowel. For example, "Carlos" becomes "Cápar-lopos." Though it's supposedly a kids' game, neither my brother nor I had ever heard of it. The fact that our parents knew about the game means it likely fell out of pop-culture relevance, since cool-kid things become lame when parents learn about them!

years this absurd Jerigonza afforded my mom and dad the ability to clandestinely communicate while my brother and I were in their presence.

It took me many years to come to appreciate, and eventually love, the qualities of the English language. And it would take even longer to concur with the wisdom of the famous Argentinian writer Jorge Luis Borges—a favorite of my dad's—who said that English (a language he had known from an early age) was a "far finer language" than his native Spanish because of what he cited as its "twin Germanic and Latin registers."

These registers, in various instances, created an ability to choose two different words to convey a single concept but in distinct ways: regal or kingly, fraternal or brotherly, dark or obscure, spirit or ghost. Borges also claimed that English was the "most physical" of languages. Expressions such as "He laughed it off" or "To live something down" simply cannot be said in the Spanish tongue.

In the end, whatever your opinion of English (or Borges), this ancient tongue of the Germanic Angles tribe, who settled Great Britain in the post-Roman period, is now our universal language. Our *lingua franca*.* At one time it was Greek, then Latin, more recently French, but today the shared language of the world is **English**. English is the mandatory means of communication between all commercial pilots and air traffic controllers on earth irrespective of their nationalities. The language of both technical writing and pop culture. Of tourism and technology. Instruction manuals and international treaties. Memes and museums.

My father loved languages and was a master of wordplay; the language of his heart was Spanish, but like so many immigrants he learned to "think" in English—an ability that served him well

* Yes, this phrase for "universal language" is composed in **Latin**, yet it literally means **French** but actually refers to **English**. Try explaining that to a kindergartner!

with his American employer. His responsibilities expanded with the ascendancy of his career, and along with that climb came a steady string of relocations for our young family. The following years would have us move in succession to Buenos Aires, Argentina; Caracas, Venezuela; and St. Thomas, US Virgin Islands—and then ultimately to Fort Lauderdale, Florida, in the mid-1980s. There I had my high school and university experiences, and there I crash-landed on an American culture that I curiously possessed yet had up until that moment never consciously experienced.

I call it a "crash landing" because returning to the United States was in many ways a shock to my young system. From a class and institutional standpoint, I had moved from a private British-American educational foundation to the Florida public school system. From the social circles of career-focused expatriates to a working-class environment in the midst of the Decade of Greed; from a traditional home and family setting that included some of the trappings of the Latin American upper classes (like live-in housekeepers, summers in the country, and the occasional chauffeur) to the reality of latch-key kids, single-parent households, and carpooling.

I was challenged to acclimate to my new surroundings; yet I had the benefits of American citizenship, fluency in English, and a good job waiting for my dad that provided for all our needs. It goes without saying that many hundreds of thousands of immigrants have nothing like those advantages. And yet all immigrants face a similar experience. A time of great change to their lived reality that must somehow be incorporated in order to flourish in a new land.

With the God-given grace of retrospect, I have come to fully understand and appreciate the beautiful gift of my own lived experience—the strangely profitable journey of a Latino Catholic kid growing up as an American expat in Latin America. At the same time I was American, Colombian, Catholic, citizen, and foreigner. A foot in many worlds.

Living in the Hyphen

There are tens of millions of people in the United States—right now—who share this experience of "living in the hyphen," of having a foot in at least two worlds and moving effortlessly between them: a bridge between the immigrant experience and the American ethos.

Those many millions of people are US Latinos, two-thirds of whom are born in this country and the majority of whom are young. I call them "200 percenters." They are 100 percent American and 100 percent Latino. They're the most significant demographic force in the United States. And, more importantly, they're

My family in Mexico, Argentina, Venezuela, US Virgin Islands, and Florida

also the future of the Catholic Church in America. Ministering to them—and through them—and the great fruit this can bear for the kingdom of God is what this book is about.

Now, one final note before we really get going. An author has in his or her mind a picture of their reader, or at least they should, and this author is no different. When I set out to write this book—a book that as I have already stated has to do in large part with the evangelical potential of the Latino population—the primary reader I first envisioned was, in fact, **not Latino**. As you read further, you will understand why that is. This doesn't mean, however, that if you **are Latino**, you should stop reading this book! On the contrary, you also will derive great value from it. In my travels, I've found that those of us who are Latino are usually as unaware of the findings in this book as are non-Latinos.

But, if you're **not Latino**, in a special way, this book is for you.

2

SPIRITUAL HEIRS OF ST. JUAN DIEGO

Most US Catholics likely have some knowledge of the miraculous claims of the appearance of Our Lady of Guadalupe nearly five hundred years ago to a poor Indigenous man on a hill in Tepeyac, Mexico. That story certainly has been covered in many ways by more informed and talented writers than yours truly. Nevertheless, I include this reference to provide an important spiritual-historical backdrop for this book: Our Lady of Guadalupe, the Patroness of the Americas, and St. Juan Diego—the witness to her apparition—play a uniquely pivotal role in the future of Catholicism here in the United States. How? Let's take a look.

Nuestra Señora de Guadalupe
(Our Lady of Guadalupe)

First, God does not partake in *coincidental* things. Nothing in God's action is incidental, let alone accidental. Rather, every one of God's thoughts and actions are full and utterly complete and entirely ordained to a specific purpose. In fact, purpose itself only exists as a reality because God is all-purposeful. So, there are no flukes where God is concerned, and nothing he does is done halfway.

It goes without saying, then, that each of us, having been personally created by God, is created for a particular time and place, not by coincidence or accident or happenstance. Not randomly, but for a reason. We are, each one of us, entirely ordained to a specific mission and also to a specific moment.

In his first homily after his election to the papacy, the late Pope Benedict XVI preached: "We are not some casual and meaningless product of evolution. Each of us is *the result of a thought of God*. Each of us is willed, each of us is loved, each of us is necessary."[1]

We are, then, to understand ourselves and one another each as an **original idea** of our Creator. And because our Creator is omnipotent, he could have chosen to have this **idea of us** at any moment in history—at any of the many instances along the line of time-space-matter that he has created.

You and I could have been born in the grasslands of Mongolia in the middle of the fifth century, or perhaps at the start of the second century in the sweep of the endless tundra of the African continent, or even (perish the thought) on some remote island archipelago one thousand years *before* the Incarnation of Christ!

But we weren't. You and I were born in either the twentieth or twenty-first century Anno Domini.* And if you're reading this book, chances are very high that you were also born in the United States or that the United States is at least your home. With a high degree of certainty, then, the person holding this book is a twentieth- or twenty-first-century American. And none of that is "just because." But why does this matter, and what does it have to do with the apparition of Our Lady of Guadalupe in Mexico nearly half a millennium ago?

I'll tell you: because each time and place has a particular people—a particular "flock," to use the Church's language. The flock is

* "In the year of our Lord." While the acronym "AD" has been replaced in many spheres with "CE" (meaning "common era"), as Christians we understand that the Incarnation of Christ in the birth of Jesus at Bethlehem is the fulcrum of history, something more easily recalled when we use the traditional term "AD."

the sum of all the people in our particular time and place. Whether they're young or old, male or female, Christian or atheist. They're our people. And the sheep of that flock must be encountered, accompanied, and deeply understood for the Church both corporately and individually to properly proclaim and live out what we call the **kerygma** in that particular time and place. So, what is this kerygma, other than a Greek term we find in the New Testament?

In simplest terms, the kerygma is *the* proclamation of our salvation in Jesus Christ. God is real. He loved you and me into existence, and he has a specific plan for you and your life—yes, you, the person holding this book—and another plan for me and my life. These plans are unique to you and me. Not just unique in the sense that yours is different from mine. But unique in the sense that your plan has never before existed, nor has mine. We're the only people for the job. But sin got in the way of these plans for our lives, so God sent his own Son to give his life in order to wipe away our sins and journey with us until we get back home to live with him in heaven, and that's really **Gospel** (Good News), so we should share it in word and action with everyone we meet!

We see examples of this kerygmatic mission to specific places and peoples throughout the pages of scripture. In the Old Testament, we see great prophets and preachers like Jonah, who was called to the people of a single city, Nineveh; Moses, who was sent to the Hebrew diaspora enslaved in Egypt; and Daniel, who encountered the people of Persia and Babylon. And in the New Testament, we see Paul of Tarsus, who was sent to the Gentiles of Syria, Asia Minor, Greece, and Rome; and Titus, who was sent to those of the island of Crete, among others.

We also see examples of this time + place + people phenomenon throughout the history of the Church itself. The great missionary saints of the Church, for example, went through profound (and often difficult) experiences in order to more intimately connect with, and be formed by, the peoples of their particular time and place: St. Francis Xavier and his namesake St. Frances Xavier Cabrini, St. Damien of Molokai, St. Junípero Serra, St. Peter

Claver, St. Patrick, and so many more. Even our new Holy Father, Leo XIV, a missionary himself, was steeped in the people and cultures of Peru, where he ministered as an Augustinian friar for more than two decades before being ordained a bishop.

But it is Jesus who gives us the best example and ultimately perfects the combination of time, place, and people. He ministered only in a very small geographic area*—roughly 150 miles north to south by 80 miles east to west—and he was "sent only to the lost sheep of the house of Israel" (Mt 15:24).

Making the kerygma relatable to a people in a particular time and place, whether they come to you, or you go to them, is called **inculturation**. It is the process of integrating the Christian faith and its liturgical, theological, and practical expressions with the cultural traditions, values, and practices of a particular community or society, while preserving the full truth of the Gospel.

It's important to note that this process of inculturation travels in both directions: Those being evangelized are enriched by the Christian message when it is delivered in a culturally relevant way, and the Christian faith itself is enriched by its new cultural expression, in turn impacting all those who then receive it, irrespective of their own cultural backgrounds.

* The primary area of Jesus's ministry (Galilee, Judea, Samaria, Perea) was within a compact region, roughly corresponding to modern-day Israel, the West Bank, and western Jordan.

† A series of Marian apparitions were reported in Kibeho, a small village in southwestern Rwanda, during the 1980s. These apparitions, recognized by the Vatican in 2001 as authentic, are the only approved Marian apparitions in Africa. The Virgin Mary's messages emphasized repentance, conversion, love, and prayer, particularly the Rosary. She urged the people of Rwanda and the world to abandon hatred, especially ethnic divisions. This was interpreted by many as a prophetic warning of the Rwandan genocide between the Hutus and Tutsis, which materialized in 1994.

Devotions to Our Lady of Knock, Lourdes, Fatima, Akita, and of course Guadalupe, along with thousands of other Catholic practices and devotions around the world, prove the two-way value of inculturation. No doubt, for example, many people in Rwanda were aided in their understanding of Christianity through an encounter with the Virgin Mary when she appeared as one of their own, Our Lady of Kibeho.[†] But even if you're not Rwandan, you can be enriched by her story, and she is now part of the patrimony of the universal Church and of your heritage as a Catholic.

The *Catechism of the Catholic Church* underscores the importance of this concept very clearly: "Missionary endeavor requires patience. . . . It must involve a *process of inculturation* if the Gospel is to take flesh in each people's culture. . . . 'With regard to individuals, groups, and peoples it is only by degrees that [the Church] touches and penetrates them and so receives them into a fullness which is Catholic'" (*CCC*, 854, emphasis added).

Nuestra Señora de Guadalupe—Our Lady of Guadalupe

In early sixteenth-century Mexico, the Blessed Virgin Mary appeared to Juan Diego, a recent convert to Christianity, in a deeply inculturated manner. Tepeyac Hill, the place where the apparition occurred in 1531, would have been revered by the Indigenous people as a sacred site dedicated to Tonantzin, an Aztec mother goddess.

The Virgin's image, later miraculously imprinted on Juan Diego's *tilma*, or cloak, depicted her with features resembling an Indigenous woman—dark skin, dark hair—and a *mestizo*, a person of mixed European and Indigenous ancestry in the former Spanish Empire. These aspects of Our Lady's appearance would have made her immediately relatable to Juan Diego and his people. Her attire also incorporated symbols of Indigenous cosmology:

- Her turquoise mantle with stars mirrored Aztec depictions of divine beings and signified the heavens.
- The black sash around her waist indicated pregnancy, aligning with Indigenous reverence for fertility and motherhood.
- The rays behind her evoked the sun, a central deity in Aztec religion, suggesting her association with the divine.

Our Lady spoke to Juan Diego in Nahuatl, his native language, validating Indigenous identity and culture, and her image contained other elements that Indigenous viewers would have understood, including

- the angel at her feet, who resembled Indigenous depictions of divine messengers; and
- the four-petal flower on her robe, which was a Nahua symbol of life, truth, and the divine presence, reinforcing her sacredness.

The subject of Guadalupe is deep and rich and profitable to study on its own. But all that aside, the fact is that Guadalupe was an inculturated experience. The reality is that God allows all apparitions of our Blessed Mother to be inculturated and thereby easily aligned with the culture of the people who experience them.

In the case of Guadalupe, she appeared to those whom Juan Diego and others would later evangelize through inculturation. This was a people who consisted of millions from among the Indigenous tribes of the storied Aztec and Mayan civilizations. In less than a decade, through Juan Diego's mission and by the grace of God and the intercession of Our Lady of Guadalupe, the majority of that flock would become Christian.

Over the ensuing decades, that Christian flock would grow, spreading far and wide, moving throughout all of Mexico, aided by Franciscan missionaries, followed by Dominicans and then Augustinians in the conversion of the Aztec kingdom. Then into

Central America: moving south through Guatemala, Honduras, and El Salvador, baptizing the ancient Mayan realm into Christianity. Then through South America—Peru, Colombia, Venezuela, Ecuador, Chile, Brazil—the same missionary religious communities would bring the truth of the Gospel of Jesus Christ and the Catholic Church to the Inca Empire.

In short order, all of Central and South America had converted. But did this great Catholic fold, which grew and spread like wildfire in the sixteenth century, remain motionless—stalled just to the south of the Tropic of Cancer? Or did these millions of newly made Christians have some bearing on the rest of "the Americas" to the north of that line? Could there be further inculturation still required? And does the story of that flock continue here in the United States even now?

To answer that question, we need to have a hard look at this flock—our flock. Who are our sheep? Who are the people of the United States of America, inside and outside the Church?

In an important sense everyone is part of the flock. In the United States, that means nearly 350 million souls from a variety of cultural, economic, and geographic backgrounds, faith walks, and ethnicities are all members of our flock. Neither Catholicism nor, even more broadly, Christianity is a prerequisite for flock membership. Recall that Christ himself proclaimed: "I have other sheep that do not belong to this fold. These also I must lead, and they will hear my voice, and there will be one flock, one shepherd" (Jn 10:16). So, yes, every American is a member of this flock. But let's go a bit deeper:

- Who has already been brought in, either by birth, marriage, or conversion, from the larger flock into our particular Catholic sheepfold?
- How does knowing these sheep intimately help us guide the rest of the flock to enter the Catholic sheepfold as well?

To explore those answers, it helps to be able to spot trends.* Trends are not foolproof, of course; ask any investor, and they'll be the first to share that past performance is no guarantee of future success. Nor is the existence of a trend an immediate indicator of a particular *cause* for the trend. Many examples throughout history show us that statistical correlation is not causation. For example, what appeared to be a straight line between sea and sky led many ancient people to erroneously conclude that the earth was flat!

And, of course, we have to remember that God is always in charge; he can intervene to stop—or even invert—a trend as he did at Tepeyac, where millions who had for centuries been trending to polytheism did a dramatic about-face and accepted belief in the God of Jesus Christ.

So now let's take a look at our trends and meet the sheep in the Catholic fold in the United States to see if things appear as we imagined.

* Simply put, spotting a trend is a way of looking at a current data signal and mapping out its trajectory on the basis of a trailing average—in other words, forecasting the future movement of a given signal based on what that signal has been observed to do over an appreciable period of time in the past.

3
OUR FLOCK

I must admit I have not always recognized what I'm about to share. It may sound counterintuitive, but just because one happens to be Latino doesn't automatically make one an expert in Latino things. My "aha moment" with respect to what was going on in our Catholic fold actually came in 2018.

By that time, I had already spent a significant portion of my professional career as an executive in the secular media industry at companies such as AOL, Walt Disney, and Univision. I studied emerging constituencies like the US Latino community and partnered with other companies to leverage the business opportunities this population presented.

Yet, if I'm being honest, it had never really occurred to me that the same dynamics that drove secular economic opportunities were in fact dramatically amplified and more urgent within the context of the Catholic Church in the United States.

One Sunday morning changed all that. I was in the sacristy of my parish vesting for my second Mass of the day (the Spanish Mass)[†] along with the celebrant priest, surrounded by lectors, altar servers, and other ministers who were coming in and out of the sacristy.

Anyone who has served in any capacity during a liturgy knows there's a liminal period in the sacristy prior to the start of the

[†] Clergy who happen to be multilingual have plenty of opportunities to serve in most dioceses. The Archdiocese of Los Angeles serves more than 4.3 million Catholics; it is the largest archdiocese in the country and third largest in the world. It has nearly three hundred parishes, and within its borders the Holy Mass is celebrated in more than forty languages every day.

celebration—a time spent preparing, reviewing readings, confirming rubrics, setting ribbons in liturgical books, and making last-minute adjustments based on the specific pastoral needs of the moment. It's only fifteen to thirty minutes, but it can be fraught with anticipation (and even anxiety) depending on the circumstances. This liminal period is also a time for brief conversations between clergy and laity, especially between priests and deacons and their altar servers.

All the altar servers in this particular parish were Latino teenagers—100 percent of them. This is not unusual, especially in Los Angeles. Our conversations were always in English, even with those who were there to serve the Spanish Mass, as on this particular Sunday. In fact, many of these young Latino altar servers didn't speak Spanish very well. A good number of them didn't speak Spanish at all. And yet there they were, faithfully, at the Spanish Mass every weekend.

At this parish, as is the case in thousands across the country, the Masses in English tended to have older parishioners and were modestly attended, while the Masses in Spanish had many young people and were generally standing room only.

I knew all these curious demographic and attendance quirks *intellectually*, but for whatever reason, I'd never intentionally remarked on or questioned the dynamic until this particular Sunday. I started a conversation with a server I'll call Manny, who was probably sixteen at the time. It went something like this:

"Manny, you don't even speak Spanish! Why are you at this Mass?" I asked.

"My family comes to this one," he said.

"I get that, but you should invite them to come to the English Mass. We could definitely use your youth there—and we need the numbers too!"

Manny laughed and went back to his preparations, but I persisted. "And it's not like that Mass doesn't count—you know the pope is OK with English, right?" I joked.

Manny paused and seemed to think about my proposition, perhaps for the first time. After a few seconds of reflection, he spoke a sentence that changed everything for me.

"No, I don't think so, Deacon. That's the white people's Mass."

Now, we need to give Manny some latitude for the inexactitude of youth. When we're young, we're prone to say things inelegantly and often with a lack of precision. Such was the case here—Manny wasn't making a reference to color at all; rather, he was referring to **culture**. I understood him immediately. In effect, he was saying, "I don't feel as comfortable in a liturgical setting that doesn't reflect my lived experience."

Here was this teenage kid who was Latino, born in the United States, who'd been coming to the Spanish Mass with his family his entire life and yet didn't really speak the language. And that's when it hit me. In an instant I flashed forward a few years to when Manny would leave his family home for university or to live on his own. The responsibility for individual Christian worship would then truly become his. If he was going to remain a practicing Catholic, he'd have to get up on Sunday mornings and worship under his own steam. What was more likely then?

Was it more likely that Manny would worship in Spanish and join a community that made him feel at home with all its cultural relevance but that did so in a language he barely understood? Where he didn't grasp the full meaning of the scriptures or intellectually grapple with the homilies? Where he'd memorized the prayers but didn't know what they meant?

Or was it more likely that he'd join a different community and worship in English, a language he understood perfectly and used everywhere—at school, in sports, on social platforms, and in conversations with friends—but that scarcely reflected his lived experience and contained none of the cultural comforts that made him feel at home? Which would Manny choose?

And the answer dawned on me. Or dropped on me, more like. Like a grand piano out of an apartment window. He'd choose *neither*. He would not worship in either setting. He'd find a different community entirely, or he might even leave the Church altogether. It was a sobering thought. Because it wasn't just about Manny. It was also about the tens of thousands—perhaps millions—of young Latino Catholics that I knew were out there and who likely were facing a similar crossroads.

But was it true? I needed to go deeper and learn if my theory was correct. In order to do that, I had to understand the American Catholic Church experience more fully. How many Latinos were in the Church? How many of them were young? Which Masses did they attend? Were they joining or leaving the Church? And why?

Figure 1. US Catholic adults by generation and race or ethnicity

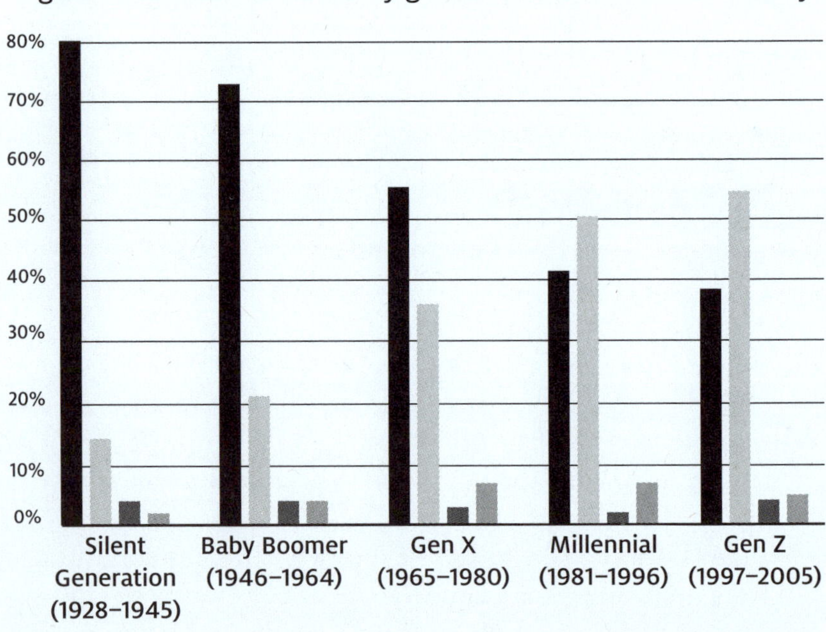

Sources: Average 2022–2023 results from Pew Research Center (2023 National Public Opinion Reference Survey), NORC at the University of Chicago (General Social Survey 1972–2022, Release 3a), Public Religion Research Institute (American Values Atlas, 2023), and Center for Applied Research in the Apostolate (CARA Catholic Poll, 2022). Data compiled by the United States Conference of Catholic Bishops.

Here's What I Found

As of 2023, between 42 and 47 percent of all self-indentified Catholics in the United States are Latino. Some educated estimates are even higher.* Two generations ago, that figure was roughly 10 percent! Said another way, since the Lyndon B. Johnson administration (or the papacy of Paul VI, take your pick), the percentage of Latino Catholics in the United States has *more than quadrupled*. And the younger you go, the more Latino the population becomes.

Today, nearly 55 percent of all Gen Z Catholics, the young people born between 1997 and 2012, are Latino, and other estimates report that more than 6 out of 10 American Catholics *under* eighteen are as well. This means that the "majority Latino" inflection point for young Catholics is already in the rearview mirror. In fact, if you're a Latino Catholic in America today, you're 257 percent more likely to be a **Zoomer** than a **boomer** (see figure 1).

But here's the really wild part, which validated my theory born out of the exchange with Manny. While all this growth of Latino Catholics has occurred, at the same time Latinos are **leading the exodus out of the Church**, and they top the ranks of the newly unaffiliated!

In August 2022, nearly 1 in 4 US Latinos in the United States was a former Catholic (see figure 2). This growing rate of defection is remarkably bad news for the Catholic composition of the Latino community in the United States. As recently as 2010, 7 out of 10 Latinos were Catholic. Today that number is closer to 4 out of 10! And the percentage of **unaffiliated** Latinos (those with no religious membership at all) has *tripled* during that same period (see figure 3).

Long story short, after all my research and study, I discovered that our **fold** contains a perfect storm of both challenge and opportunity. A reality summed up in a simple, yet boggling paradox: **Every day the Catholic Church in the United States shrinks but has more Latinos, while simultaneously the US Latino population grows but has fewer Catholics!**

This seemingly incongruous statement highlights the statistical irony that the Catholic Church in the United States is becoming increasingly Latino, but the Latino population in the United States is becoming increasingly less Catholic. At the same time. Latinos each day are a larger share *within* the Church, but fewer Latinos overall are *remaining* in the Church.

It's difficult to overstate the importance of this paradoxical dilemma and the urgency it clearly creates: The truth is that the Catholic Church, both institutionally and by way of the individual and corporate actions of her parishes and many apostolates, has a **blind spot**.

For many decades, as a Church, we've attempted to encounter and serve the Latino population largely through Spanish liturgies and translations, but transformational strategies for lasting engagement, accompaniment, and integration have been sorely lacking. And this shows in the numbers. But make no mistake, this is not a one-way dynamic. Those of us who are Latino Catholics share

Figure 2. Religious switching among US Latino adults

	Childhood religion	Current religion	Left religion	Joined religion
Protestant	18%	21%	6%	9%
Catholic	65	43	23	1
Other Christian	2	1	1	1
Other faiths	1	2	<1*	2
Religiously unaffiliated	13	30	3	20

**Does not include respondents who moved between non-Christian faiths.*

Source: Pew Research Center's National Survey of Latinos conducted August 1–14, 2022.

in some of the cause for the predicament we're in. Many Latinos, in light of the lack of real engagement, have regrettably sequestered themselves in Latino parishes, hyperlocalized their Catholic experience to the Spanish Mass, or siloed themselves exclusively within Hispanic ministries.

On the opposite end of the spectrum, many Latino Catholics have assimilated* to such an extent, by choice or because of isolation, that any cultural distinctives they may have had to contribute

Figure 3. Religious affiliation of US Latino adults

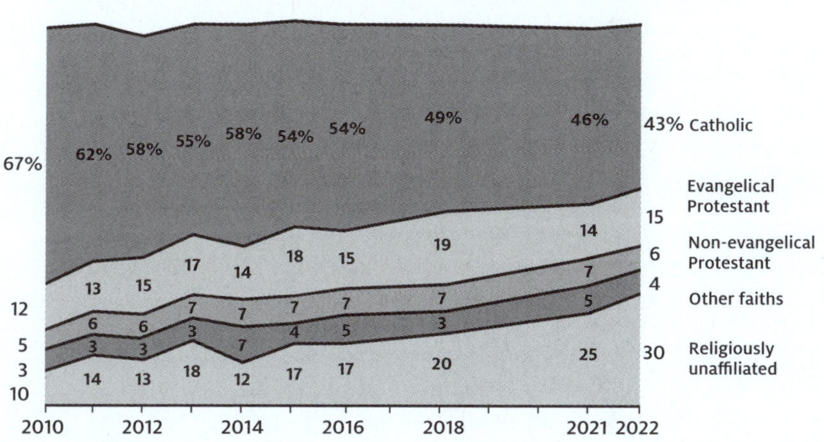

Source: Pew Research Center's National Survey of Latinos, 2010–2016, 2018, 2021–2022.

* **Assimilation** is the absorption of the attributes of a dominant culture by someone, usually an immigrant or their descendants. It is distinct from **acculturation**. Assimilation indicates a loss of cultural distinctiveness over time, whereas acculturation entails an incorporation or "layering on" of new attributes on top of the existing dominant ones—often creating a new reality (e.g., in recent years American pop music has been so influenced by Latin genres—regional Mexican, reggaeton, salsa, etc.—that it and its biggest stars have been reshaped).

to the Church have been lost to history. Still others, wittingly or unwittingly, have anesthetized their personal agency by subscribing to outdated cultural mores that keep them stuck "in their lane" (*Calladita te ves más bonita!**).

Now, imagine if all of this was happening outside of the Church in the secular world—in business, politics, or entertainment. What would happen then? How would those industries respond?

As a media and marketing professional, I can't help but think how this "perfect storm" of risk and opportunity would be handled within a secular business environment, where a bias in favor of market share, margins, and money rules the day and provides singular operational clarity. Let's try a little thought experiment.

Let's pretend you're on the board of a Fortune 500 company, a public company the likes of Apple or Amazon, Target or Toyota. In a board meeting, the CEO shockingly confesses to you and the other board members that for years his team has overlooked nearly *half* of the company's market.

And this particular half of its customers—whom they have been ignoring—happens to be the one segment of the market that is driving all the growth in the category and is quite literally the future of the entire industry.

Oh, and finally, imagine that the CEO further states that in order to fix this massive oversight and make up for the tens of billions of dollars in lost market capitalization, he will now institute a strategy to increase sales by translating the instruction manuals of all their products!

* This is an old refrain, likely originating in Mexico and often taught to young girls. It literally means "You look prettier when you're quiet." It's the rough equivalent of "Kids should be seen, not heard," but with a dash of machismo thrown in for good measure. In many cases, the net result is a docility not rooted in Christian virtue but instead based on a type of cultural blindness to important issues because they are "beyond my station" or "none of my business."

As a board member, what would you do? After picking yourself up off the floor and gathering your composure, you'd likely suggest much more than a new strategy. You'd recommend a new CEO. And you'd be right to do so. Fiduciary responsibility—*and common sense*—would dictate that the CEO should be relieved of his duties. ASAP.

But we all know that the likelihood of the example above actually occurring is vanishingly small. No secular CEO worth their salt would allow half their prospective market to entirely escape their attention. In the secular business world there are simply too many incentives tied to growth and market share; too many eyes watching the bottom line; too many board members, investors, and shareholders ready to fire off concerned emails; too many ambitious executives on the inside trying to crack new markets in order to gain promotion; too many competitors trying to steal market share. There is simply no chance that an entire market opportunity that was in all respects available, accessible, and winnable would simply be overlooked. That just wouldn't happen.

And yet, in the Church, this kind of thing happens every day. To be clear, by this I do not mean that bishops, clergy, employees, volunteers, and parishioners throughout our country are not aware of the Latino population in the pews of America's churches—they are. We are. And many fruitful ministries, in parishes and elsewhere, exist that have been a blessing in the lives of many Latinos. No, we're definitely aware of our Latino brothers and sisters. We see them, speak to them, preach to them, and minister to them. And, of course, we translate for them.

But I suggest—fully aware of the controversy this may create—that, generally speaking, current pastoral and other ecclesial efforts toward engaging US Latinos are largely

- **reactive**: not intentional, strategic, or organized; and
- **generic**: not informed by lived experience but instead "one size fits all."

And here lies the great opportunity! An opportunity that the secular world across politics, business, media, and pop culture long ago seized and mobilized. We have an opportunity now to take a page out of their playbook and "baptize" their strategies, as we've done so many times in our Christian past. And what a blessing this can be since our currency, unlike the world's, isn't speeches, stock prices, or sales—but *souls*!

Among the great ironies in the journey of faith is witnessing how God can use the unexpected as an object lesson for spiritual growth: in this case, how the secular world, whose ultimate end is better economics, efficiency, or market share, can nevertheless illustrate for us Christians a more focused and responsive model of how to "evangelize" and "convert"!*

In the final analysis, when we consider all the demographic trends from the troubling vantage point of an overall shrinking of Christian adherence and practice in the United States (see figure 4)—a reality suggesting that our century may be the last for Christianity as a meaningful cultural force in America—we do not have to be futurists to conclude that, should our current trajectory hold, the US Catholic Church of tomorrow will be a smaller, overwhelmingly *Latino* Church.

This book, among other things, proposes that neither smaller nor overwhelmingly Latino is what anyone (especially Catholics!) should want for the Church in the United States. We shouldn't want a smaller Church, of course, but rather we should want our churches to overflow as we fulfill the Great Commission and help *every soul* in our flock enjoy the fullness of a saving relationship with Jesus Christ and his Church (see Matthew 28:16–20).

* In my professional career at firms like Walt Disney and Univision, I heard terminology like this every day—usually from non-Christians. In fact, garnering a new customer in any marketing context is called a "conversion."

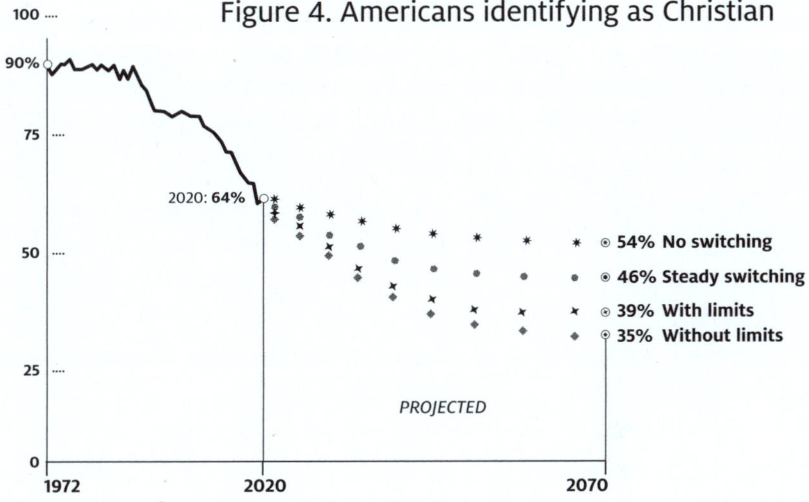

No switching
This scenario imagines no person in American has changed or will change their religion after 2020.

Steady switching
Movement into and out of Christianity remains stable at recently observed rates. That is, in each new generation, 31% of Christians become religiously unaffiliated before they turn 30, and 21% of unaffiliated people become Christian.

Rising disaffiliation <u>with</u> limits
In each new generation, a growing share of Christians switch out before they turn 30, while a shrinking share of "nones" switch in. But the switching rate is capped to prevent the share of Christians who leave the faith from rising above 50%.

Rising disaffiliation <u>without</u> limits
In each new generation, a growing share of Christians switch out before they turn 30, while a shrinking share of "nones" switch in. No cap is imposed on switching rates.

Sources: Pew Research Center's General Social Survey 1972–2006, Pew Research Center 2007–2021 surveys, and Pew Research Center 2020–2070 projections.

Note: Historical data describes trends among US adults based on surveys of adults. The 2020 estimate and subsequent projections show Americans of all ages based on the estimate that the religious composition of people of all ages roughly matches the adult composition.

Nor should we want an overwhelmingly Latino church—because as members of the **Katholikos** (καθολικός) or Universal Church, in the most "universal" country the world has ever known, our fold should be the very embodiment of the many rich cultural expressions of our nation weaving their own unique fabric into the tapestry of American Catholicism.

In short, I propose that it is the Latino community that has a unique role to play in reversing America's troubling trends and in ensuring the survival and the future thriving of the Catholic Church in the United States. And I'm not alone. Some of the most influential episcopal voices agree.

The archbishop of Los Angeles, His Excellency José H. Gómez, in a prophetic turn of phrase, observed in a homily at a gathering of national Latino leaders that Latinos in the United States are truly the "spiritual heirs of Juan Diego."* That's a big deal.

Latinos have inherited their mission directly from St. Juan Diego. The mission that the Lord entrusted to him through his mother, Mary, which led tens of millions to the gift of Christianity, continues. It continues in *this* America. In *our* America. Right here. Right now.

Unless those of us who are Latino recognize the spiritual inheritance we've received from Guadalupe and know that we've been entrusted with continuing the mission of Juan Diego to convert all of the Americas to Christ, we will not succeed. And unless those of us who are *not* Latino recognize that our efforts,

* "The Virgin entrusted St. Juan Diego with a mission—she sent him to go and tell the [local] bishop to build a church for our Lord. . . . Jesus called a lay person to be first, to lead his mission in the Americas. Brothers and sisters, you are the children of Guadalupe, *Guadalupanos*; you are the spiritual heirs of Juan Diego. The mission entrusted to him, is now entrusted to you." From the homily of Archbishop José H. Gómez at the closing Mass of the V Encuentro, 2018.

ministries, apostolates, and gifts are incomplete if we do not thoughtfully integrate them with, and for, our Latino brothers and sisters in a meaningful way, we will not succeed.

I hope by now you are beginning to see that "having a Spanish Mass" at your parish or "translating a website" are desperately insufficient means both practically and pastorally to be truly kerygmatic in our particular time and place—insufficient to fully proclaim and live the Gospel in the United States of America. We must do what we can to stop treating Latino ministry as a side apostolate but view it instead as the **central vineyard** of the Church's future in the United States.

4

DEI AND ALL THAT

Let's address something that as a faithful Christian you might already be thinking—especially if you're **not Latino**. Isn't all of this focus on someone's ethnicity a bad thing? Aren't we all children of God, and doesn't the overemphasis on ethnic identity tend to sow discord and division? Also, isn't all this ethnic and racial interest actually at the heart of social and political ideologies that are ultimately *antagonistic* to the Catholic faith and against the Gospel?

Yes and no. *No tires lo bueno por lo malo.** Yes, of course all baptized people are first and foremost children of God (see 1 John 3:1). Our dignity as human persons both precedes—and supersedes—any characteristic of culture, class, or color. Too much emphasis on our particular ethnicity can be misunderstood, or purposely misused, and in effect can result in a kind of balkanization—where we only relate to one another, or worse, we only associate with one another, as a result of membership within a particular group. That is definitely *not* Catholic.

Over the last two decades in the West, and especially in our country, there has been a marked emphasis on investments, social platforms, and "virtue signaling" around diversity initiatives from politicians, corporations, brands, and celebrities. The speed and similarity of these initiatives left many with the impression that they were the product of a trending news cycle rather than the fruit of thoughtful discernment, and many were unmoored from any foundation of lasting virtue.

* Though not a word-for-word translation, this is the idiomatic equivalent of "Don't throw the baby out with the bathwater."

Reinforced by the chatter of the political class and the punditry of social media influencers, this period created a disorienting avalanche of publicity, protests, and policies that excited some as much as they bewildered others. An entire alphabet soup of vernacular subsequently arose; most germane to our discussion was the surge in popularity of the term "DEI."

Standing for "diversity, equity, and inclusion," the acronym DEI is not new. It solidified in the early 2000s, particularly in corporate, educational, and governmental contexts. By the 2010s, DEI had become a standard framework in human resources and organizational policies, driven in part by globalization, workforce demographic changes, and studies stating that diverse teams improved innovation and therefore performance. The unrest and protests of 2020 dramatically amplified DEI's prominence, with organizations committing to initiatives to address systemic racism and inequality. What should a well-formed Catholic perspective make of all this? And how does the answer impact the rest of this book?

Recall that the Catholic Church rejects nothing that is true irrespective of the source. Since Jesus Christ is Truth Incarnate (see 1 John 5:20), and since all truth flows from the life of the Divine Trinity, then to the extent that something is true, it ultimately has its origin in God. If it is not true, then it is, by definition, not of God.

And the truth is that notwithstanding some modern misperceptions and mischaracterizations, diversity is a **good** that has been built into the truth of creation itself—a gift from God, who is Truth. Diversity is everywhere: from the geological and material diversity of our planet's substrate, to the diversity of climates spread throughout the various planets of our solar system, to the diversity of peoples of the earth each with their own language, music, art, and culture. It follows, then, that each cultural background and ethnic experience has gifts to bear for the People of God and a part to play in the divine plan. The *Catechism of the Catholic Church* lays it out quite nicely:

> From the beginning, this one Church has been marked by a great diversity which comes from both the variety of God's gifts and the diversity of those who receive them. Within the unity of the People of God, a multiplicity of peoples and cultures is gathered together. . . . The great richness of such diversity is not opposed to the Church's unity. (*CCC*, 814)

That last line is key. Diversity, from a Christian perspective, should never be esteemed for its own sake, but rather as a reality that is only made complete, and thus achieves its fullness, within the context of **unity**.

A friend of mine, José Manuel De Urquidi—a leader in the area of Latino Catholic thought and a full participant at the Synod on Synodality in Rome—recently shared a never-before-seen message given to him by Pope Francis of happy memory.

Facing José Manuel De Urquidi's iPhone camera, Pope Francis speaks on diversity and unity.

The Holy Father, in his inimitable way, spoke directly into José Manuel's iPhone camera and illustrated in a few quick lines how diversity should properly be understood. Pope Francis warned, "Difference only makes sense when it is unified. . . . Variety without unity is not Christian, and unity without variety is like a museum."

In the end, as is the case with all Catholic things, questions of culture, language, and demography are not either-or but rather both-and propositions. A healthy Catholic understanding says that we should hold preeminent the reality of the ***Imago Dei*** (that is, the image and likeness of God) and our common bond as members of the human family, irrespective of our background or ethnicity, while at the same time honoring and seeking to better understand our various cultural expressions and experiences, especially those of our given flock, in order to achieve a broader and deeper evangelization and create a greater unity.

5
WHAT MAKES LATINOS DIFFERENT?

OK, you might say—I get all that. I'm with you so far. I understand the demographic urgency, and I even understand the spiritual and religious dimensions. But what I don't get is what makes the Latino population different from the various other immigrant groups of the American past—such as the Dutch, German, Eastern European, Italian, Polish, Irish, African, and Asian populations.

Perhaps you yourself have European, African, or Asian heritage and can't recall any special approaches or ministerial strategies for your particular cultural background. Why, then, would we choose to focus on the Latino opportunity in a different way? Why should we pay special attention to Latinos?

Four key factors make the Latino experience in America worthy of focused consideration:

1. **Population size**: orders of magnitude larger
2. **Technology**: digitally enabled community
3. **Media**: abundance of inculturated content offerings
4. **Travel**: democratization of international tourism

Let's start with population size. In 2024, the total Latino population in the United States, including US-born citizens, legal immigrants, and undocumented migrants, was between 66 and 72 million.[1] This represents somewhere between 19 and 21 percent of the total US population of 340 million. So, **one of every five people living in America right now is Latino.**

This means that the US Latino population is five to six times larger than the combined total of all the immigrants who arrived via Ellis Island and other New York ports of entry in the late nineteenth and early twentieth centuries.* Numbers of Latinos in the United States are simply orders of magnitude larger than any previous wave of European, African, or Asian immigration America has seen—and they're growing faster than almost every other demographic group in the country. The US Census projects the Latino population will be roughly a third of the total US population by 2060. This fact sheds new light on the dubious assertion that this community should be seen in the same way as previous waves of immigration, which lacked the same volumetric advantage.

Second, technology plays a significant role, especially the myriad personal and group communication technologies (social media, WhatsApp, VoIP, native video-calling apps, etc.) that were unthinkable in the Ellis Island days. These technologies create, among other things, the ability to build one-on-one relationships and establish community more broadly, enabling Latinos to remain deeply connected to the people and culture of their homeland.

Compare that to the prospects of an early twentieth-century immigrant from Poland, for example. The only way that person might communicate with other Poles or retain their sense of Polish community was within their own homes and to the extent they resided in a "Polish neighborhood."

Connected to this technological reality is the third important factor, the present-day superabundance of media and content choices made available through many of the same platforms

* Historical records from the National Park Service and Migration Policy Institute indicate that approximately 12 million immigrants were processed through Ellis Island between 1892 and 1954, with the vast majority (around 10–11 million) arriving between 1892 and 1924, the peak years.

already mentioned. I recall once, years ago, on a whim deciding to watch a Bollywood movie on my Netflix account, only to later discover that the algorithm had whipped up an entire *shelf* of Indian film fare for me to consume upon my next visit. Had I wanted to, I could have spent the next decade bingeing Indian movies and TV series across every genre conceivable. Had I happened to be Indian, this massive content availability and exposure would certainly have enabled me to retain a stronger connection to my Indian heritage.

Now think again about our Polish immigrant friend from the Ellis Island of the 1920s. The only way he might have interacted with "Polish media" would have been to the extent he had access to a regional Polish magazine, listened to a Polish announcer on a radio show, or read a local Polish newspaper in the borough in which he resided. And if he happened to leave New York and head west, as many did, he would have quickly snuffed out even the meager Polish content offering that he had access to in New York City.

The final differentiating factor between modern US Latinos and previous waves of American immigrants is the ease and democratization of travel. Plentiful flight options, low-cost carriers, and an explosion of global aviation routes have changed the immigrant experience forever.

According to the US Bureau of Transportation, in any given month nearly forty thousand commercial flights depart the United States bound for Mexico and other destinations in Latin America.[2] Among the passengers on those forty thousand flights are *millions* of Latinos visiting their birth countries or ancestral homelands (just as I did as a kid when I visited my extended family in Colombia). This ability to interact and immerse physically in a culture and language creates a heritage-retention ability unlike anything that was possible in the early twentieth century.

When our Polish friend from the 1920s left Warsaw to board a steamship, likely docked in Hamburg or Amsterdam and bound for the New York harbor, he was leaving not for a two-week vacation, or for a summer abroad, but for his *entire life*. The odds of his being able to return to Poland for a visit with the family were extraordinarily low. This is clearly not the case for today's immigrants.

As a result of these four factors, and presumably others, the typical journey of assimilation (the historical notion of a melting pot), whereby immigrants, or their US-born descendants, simply blend in by learning the language and "becoming American," has long since evolved. I've heard it said that rather than a melting pot, the experience of US immigration today is better likened to a salad bowl. We have referred to this as **acculturation**—the layering by immigrants of new-to-them American experiences upon those cultural habits, traditions, perceptions, and ways of relating from their home cultures, retaining all of these things in unison.

Whatever you choose to call the evolution of American immigration, what is evident is that fundamental changes have indeed occurred. Yet our ministerial approaches and strategies have not evolved to keep pace with the landscape of modern immigration. In many ways, as regards the Gospel opportunity, we're still stuck in the 1920s.

So, this has been quite a buildup! But what can we actually do about all this? Well, it takes more than tactics. And it certainly takes more than translating a language! It takes prayer. It takes a desire to encounter. It takes a strategy. And all good strategies begin with an **insight**.

6

THE POWER OF INSIGHTS

Now, here's a curious thing. With all this talk about Latinos, the word "insight," which is the seedbed of any winning strategy and what we will be exploring through the rest of this book, actually has no direct translation in Spanish!

I recall being annoyed and frustrated in a conversation with my mom—whose Spanish (both diction and grammar) is exceptionally deep and refined—when I tried in vain to explain what the heck an insight was. Not being able to find the translation in the stores of my mind, I ultimately settled on the lame description *una gran idea* (a really big idea) and on a tongue-twisting portmanteau (a word blending the sounds and combining the meanings of two others), *innovador-idea* (innovative + idea).

And yet it was precisely because of this missing Spanish translation that many years ago on a business trip to Mexico City, I first understood what strange and powerful things insights actually are.

My work at the time, as the head of a large division at a major media company, meant striking and implementing deals with media executives in Latin America, often working with business-unit heads, strategists, marketers, and their external partners and agencies in the country. In meeting after meeting, peppered throughout our many conversations would often appear particular words in English. These words in English were generally related to specific genres or topics—pop culture, business administration, technology, innovation—along with marketing concepts like start-ups, branding, crowdfunding, streaming. All decidedly American things.

What these Mexican professionals were speaking wasn't Spanglish* in a strict sense. Rather than using an English word to create relatability or out of ignorance of the correct Spanish word, as is the case with Spanglish, my counterparts were using the English word intentionally as a contextualizer—a comprehension tool without which the idea being communicated would fall apart in its entirety.

Chief among these English words scattered throughout our many conversations was "insight." My Mexican friends used this word excitedly, explicitly, and repeatedly. They used it to describe something unique and more than the sum of its parts. It was a fresh discovery. An idea that could give birth to other things. A root concept that could serve as the basis for whole new strategies or product lines or market directions. They used it as a word that opened up new frontiers. A word that implied a method to short-circuit the status quo.

I had of course heard the word "insight"—and used it—before. But until that point, to the extent that I had used it, I had done so lazily: maybe as a synonym for "clever" or "profound" (and it is those things). But because of the way my Mexican colleagues were using the word, and because it stood alone in the conversation contrasted by Spanish, I heard it almost as if for the very first time.

It turned out that an **insight** was something very special indeed. And on reflection, it seemed to contain a few key ingredients that separated it from garden-variety ideas, discoveries, or concepts. I began to understand that insights

- were mined, or discovered, from observable data;

* A portmanteau that has entered the American vernacular, meaning a mix of Spanish and English. In practice, however, Spanglish is usually employed in two very different ways: (1) by Latinos who, when speaking in English, occasionally use words in Spanish for emphasis or to create relatability with other Latinos, or (2) by Latinos who don't speak Spanish fluently but who can communicate basic concepts to Spanish-dominant listeners through interpolation.

- were often hiding in plain sight;
- contained a human truth;
- often brought about a change in the previous thought trajectory; and
- gave birth to a variety of new opportunities and applications.

Like buying a new car you thought was one-of-a-kind only to then see it everywhere after driving off the lot, I started to see insights all around me after that trip to Mexico! I saw insights in business proposals, in works of art, and certainly in new brands and products.

One such example I studied was the insight that gave birth to the mobile mapping app Waze. The entire value proposition of this global technology brand was rooted in a singular insight that upended years of orthodox thinking in the development of mapping software. It was bewilderingly simple: **Consumers don't care how far away it is; they only care how long it takes to get there.**

Boom. Insight! Born of data. Hiding in plain sight. Based on a human truth. Changes the previous direction. Gives birth to a variety of new opportunities and applications. You see, all the other mapping apps and software had been developed and were being optimized for distance. How far away was the destination? Was that in miles or kilometers? What was the best combination of streets and configuration of turns to minimize the distance? But this new app, Waze, would instead develop its technology and optimize its service for time! Genius. Waze would tell the user the *fastest* way to get where they were going, not necessarily the shortest way. A radical idea, but one instantly obvious, clear, and relatable. And a star was born. A star that (despite occasionally directing users to drive down alleys or take dangerous left turns across four lanes of traffic) was sold to Google only a few years later for $1.15 billion and is today worth multiples of that sum and used by more than 140 million drivers every month.

Netflix provides us with another example of insight fueling innovation. Inspired by local video stores that dealt in bulky VHS tapes, rental fees, and purchases, the originators of the now-ubiquitous streaming giant discovered that **most people didn't want to own (or even rent) VHS tapes or DVDs; they just wanted to watch movies and shows at home**. Of course! Consumers didn't need to own *Indiana Jones and the Temple of Doom* or *Casablanca*; they just wanted access to it! Based on that foundational insight, Netflix built a novel subscription model and workflow that allowed a steady stream of movies and shows to be delivered to a consumer's door via snail mail, and eventually directly to their televisions via the internet. Today, the company famously claims its "only competition is sleep." It boasts 240 million subscribers (with another 250 million sharing passwords!), streams 6 billion hours of content each month, makes more movies than any Hollywood studio, and, at a market capitalization of $485 billion, is nearly three times the size of traditional media companies such as Disney.

But there is a far more ancient example of insight—one that draws us much closer to the spiritual dimension and has much to tell us about the true origin of insights. The ancient Greek mathematician Archimedes famously jumped out of his bath and ran naked through the streets of Athens screaming, "I found it!" after being hit by this spiritual reality. What happened to him might be called an epiphany—a discovery based on data, hidden right under his nose, that changed the direction of things.

Despite his prodigious intellect and mathematical prowess, Archimedes had been obsessing about a problem he could not solve. The king of Syracuse had asked him to determine if a golden crown the king had received was genuine or if it had been adulterated by an unscrupulous goldsmith. Archimedes considered ways to solve the dilemma, but after days of straining his brain for answers and finding none, he gave up and decided instead to go to the public bathhouse for a dip, hoping a warm plunge might soothe his frustration.

Stepping into the tub, Archimedes noticed that the water level rose as it was displaced by his body. At that moment came a great insight: **He could measure the volume of the crown by the amount of water it displaced, and then, comparing it to the weight of the crown, he could determine its density.** Archimedes knew the density of gold, so any deviation from that density would indicate that another metal had been mixed into the crown, rendering it a fake.

Archimedes's epiphany illuminated what was previously unclear. It was a sudden realization, a new understanding—profound and transformative. This was a proverbial "aha moment," when a concept, truth, or meaning clicks into place—a breakthrough. An insight like this brings a sense of clarity and revelation accompanied by a feeling of great surprise or excitement.

Armed with our Christian imagination, we can build on this by recalling the greatest epiphany. A moment of supreme manifestation. A moment based on observable data, which was discovered and revealed, was rooted in a human truth, and changed the direction of all things. The true epiphany—the ultimate revelation, the ultimate manifestation, the ultimate insight: the Incarnation and birth of Our Lord Jesus Christ.

Insights, properly understood, are good things—things of God. They are far more valuable in the development of wisdom than recommendations, suggestions, tips, or best practices. Why? Because all of those things, though potentially helpful, may nevertheless not work in your particular circumstances. Consider:

- Does a best practice of which fork to use in dining etiquette have bearing in an Ethiopian context, where cutlery is typically not employed to eat?
- Is a recommendation for achieving TikTok sales virality relevant for the marketing director of a nursing home who is trying to reach senior citizens with her advertising?
- Does a suggestion for a typical weekend getaway apply in an Islamic culture that doesn't observe Saturday and Sunday as days of rest from work?

Well, no, of course not.

Insights, however, are far different. They always apply, are always relevant. Insights are not detached, discrete things. They're not things you execute, implement, or build; rather, they are avenues that can be traveled in order to **inspire an idea** that fits your unique set of circumstances, in your specific location, and in a way tailored to your needs.

Here's my hope and prayer for you and the remainder of this book: that in your hands, dear reader, the insights outlined in the following section will detonate a unique idea, concept, or approach that can work in your particular slice of the world for the growth of the Church and the greater glory of God!

But before we go further, I want to highlight one general point that will be reflected in the insights I'm about to share: The Latino population in the United States is young. A whole generation younger than the average population, in fact. The mean age for a Latino in the United States is thirty-eight. It's forty-eight for a non-Latino person. To that end, the insights that follow are particularly informed by younger folks. That's not to say the insights don't apply to older Latinos—they do—but their greatest impact and resonance will be seen with respect to millennials and younger. And that's a good thing. The youth of this nation are the future of the Church, and we should all be looking for ways to better connect with, and relate to, the next generation of believers—no matter who they are!

So, at last, we arrive at the meat and potatoes—*el arroz con pollo**—of this book. What are the insights pertaining to the Latino community in the United States? What are those transferable, adaptable, exportable avenues of ideation and innovation that can be learned and then unlocked within your given ministerial circumstances, and how can you use them? Here we go!

* Not a translation, but a transcreation. You'll learn more about transcreations in the discussion of insight 2.

PART II
Insights

Insight 1

GO *THROUGH* LATINOS, NOT JUST *TO* LATINOS

If it's relatable to Latinos, especially younger ones, they'll amplify it to everyone else.

In 2016, when I was working as an executive at a technology–digital media start-up, I was involved in a partnership with Pricewaterhouse-Coopers, a large secular consulting firm. Together we conducted a study to determine the relative diversity of an American millennial's social media network. We were trying to understand the composition of the social networks of young people in the United States to analyze how they were sharing social content and with whom. We queried and tracked one thousand millennials from a variety of ethnic backgrounds to get at the answers. The results were fascinating.

What we observed was that the **engagement** on social platforms (measured as comments, likes, and, most importantly, shares) among eighteen- to thirty-four-year-olds was fairly similar among most ethnic cohorts, with one notable exception—Latinos. If you were Anglo* or Black and between eighteen and thirty-four

* I'm choosing the designation "Anglo" instead of "White," not because I think there's anything wrong with using the latter, but to more closely match the counterpart term "Latino." For our purposes, it is more apropos to use a term that relates to folks descended principally from Europeans (Anglo), just as we have for folks descended principally from Latin Americans (Latino). Also, there are lots of White Latinos. And finally, the term is appropriate here because "Anglo" connotes English speaking.

years old, the composition of your social media footprint looked a lot like you. Said another way, if you were Black or Anglo, by and large the folks that you were connected to, and were engaging with, on Instagram and Facebook shared your ethnicity. But the social footprints of Latino young people showed a very different pattern: Not only did they have a significantly higher concentration of Latinos in their networks, but they also displayed a higher composition of each of the other ethnic groups, yielding much greater overall diversity.

This meant that for the purposes of social media connectivity, the eighteen-to-thirty-four-year-old Latino was, in effect, a type of superconnector. If properly activated, they could detonate and help transmit a message through the social ecosystem faster than others within the same age cohort but of different ethnicities.

This finding meant, among other things, that when US Latino eighteen- to thirty-four-year-olds shared something on social media, they were automatically amplifying that message to a broad

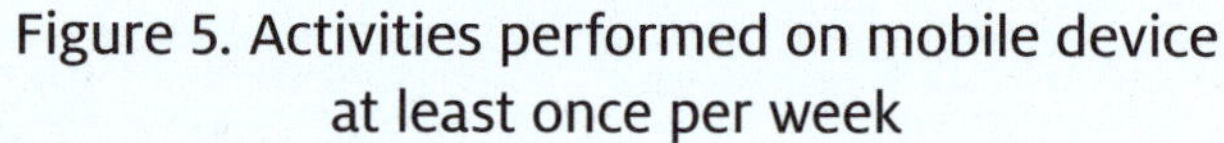
Figure 5. Activities performed on mobile device at least once per week

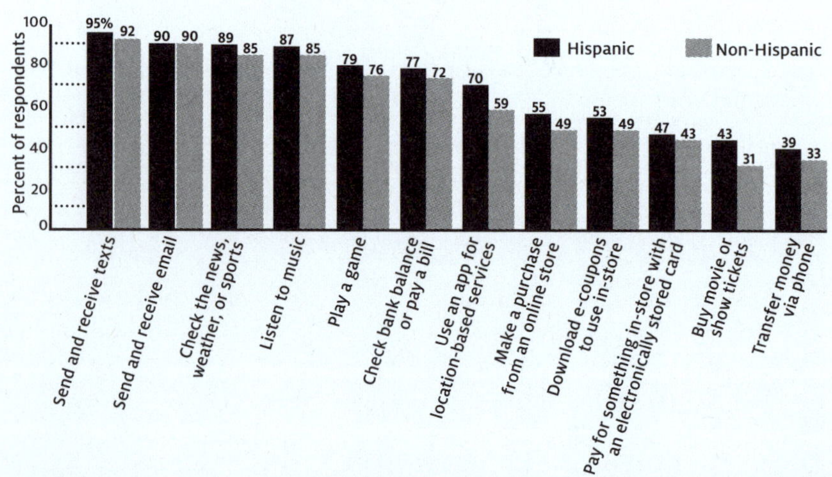

Source: PricewaterhouseCoopers survey of 1,000 Hispanic consumers conducted July 2016.

and diverse group of people. Therefore, when developing content or advertising with this young Latino consumer in mind, producers had to consider not only what message was going to be relevant and valuable to them directly but also how that same message might be made valuable to the **secondary audience** that would receive the content through sharing.

Most importantly, the Latino young people in our study displayed a higher propensity to be active on social platforms to begin with. They had a higher rate of engagement, shared more often, and made more comments. They simply seemed in most respects and across most metrics to be more energized and active. Many of these same characteristics continue to exist in a measurable way today (see figure 5).

Younger Latinos in effect possess a built-in bonus feature for those of us engaged in the evangelizing mission of the Church. They bring more bang for the evangelical buck! If you engage them authentically, through them the message can be carried forward to others, both Latinos and non-Latinos alike. In fact, the more specific and relevant to Latinos the content or advertising is, the more universal the distribution of that content is likely to be. Universality through specificity is a key feature of this insight.

The information we gathered and the insight we gained from this study led to a series of interesting implications. For example, the choice of language for content or advertising delivery to young Latinos could no longer be oversimplified. If the content or advertising was relevant and engaging, then Latinos would share it more often than non-Latinos, and when they did, they would be sharing it across ethnicities and languages more often. So, we could no longer rely on simply using Spanish to reach this Latino consumer, especially if we wanted to be relevant to the people that the message would be shared with. We'd be leaving value on the table if we didn't attend to this straightforward reality. Based on implications like these, a number of strategies and tactics emerged in the secular world that we can now draw inspiration from in our church systems, organizational structures, and pastoral outreach efforts. One such strategy has been the creation of advertising and content experiences designed to resonate authentically with Latinos even though they are delivered exclusively in English.

In 2017 and 2021 respectively, the Walt Disney Company released the films *Coco* and *Encanto*. The first of these animated movies was set in Mexico and the second in Colombia, and both featured authentic storylines, characters, cultural traditions, and music from those communities. Before you assume that the making of those films was some faux altruistic political statement designed to virtue-signal to the Latino community, let me assure you of the contrary. I was a senior executive at Walt Disney for many years, and I can tell you from personal experience within that corporate culture that these films would never have been green-lit had their economic promise been truly limited to the Latino community alone. Never. Disney, like any other corporate media entity, is principally driven by economic success and competitive aspiration.

Disney saw that if it could create a movie that would authentically resonate with Latino audiences, then through these same audiences, it could amplify and drive relevance to everyone else. And the company was right.

Both films were box-office successes, generating collectively more than $1.1 billion in ticket sales alone—not to mention the combined successes of their music soundtracks, merchandise, experiential sales, and subscription revenue generated via streaming audiences on Disney+. They were massive multi-billion-dollar hits.

Universality through specificity. Can you imagine the Gospel potential of a similar strategy?

Discard Previous Ways of Thinking

- Avoid the false dichotomy between "English-speaking" and "Spanish-speaking" definitions and ministries. Most Latinos belong to both worlds, and neither exclusively.
- A Latino idea, story, or concept can be the centerpiece for an overall strategy, approach, or initiative to reach all consumer groups.
- The more authentic and relevant a piece of Latino online content or advertising is, the more it will generate a broader secondary audience that may or may not speak Spanish.
- Social media has an incremental and accelerated value with Latinos in the United States, particularly younger ones.

What Next?

- Have I executed a simple research study of the Latino families in my parish or faith community to understand their background and needs?
- Have I fulfilled a Sunday obligation by attending the Spanish Mass and used that as a means to meet the Latino community in my parish and better understand their needs, especially those of the young people?
- Have I explored and gleaned information and insight from examples of Latino-focused marketing or business strategies from the secular world and tested them in a ministerial setting?

Insight 2

LANGUAGE IS A TOOL; CULTURE IS A GATEWAY

Context, culture, and lived experience are more important than language in driving relatability and connection.

I remember the first time I came across a video of Fr. Agustino Torres on YouTube. I was a few weeks away from filming a TED Talk–style presentation at a soundstage about an hour south of Minneapolis organized by the Catholic media company Our Sunday Visitor.

In preparation for the day of recording, I had checked out the other speakers online—notable Catholic evangelists, heads of apostolates, and thought leaders from all over the country. Among them was an infectiously jovial Franciscan friar named Fr. Agustino. I should note that I paid special attention to his online profile because in my experience at that time, and to this day, it was unusual to find other Catholic Latinos in national public-ministry settings, especially in an English-first context.

I found out that Fr. Agustino was a member of the Franciscan Friars of the Renewal, an order based in the Bronx, New York, and was a well-traveled preacher and speaker. He had been born in South Texas, a border kid with a Mexican family. Now he was living in New York City and carried out his various ministries in largely Latino precincts.

My research also led me to a series of videos of a very well-attended Latino youth conference in Los Angeles at which he preached. The crowd was several thousand teens and young adults gathered in an amphitheater setting with concert-like lighting and atmospherics. Fr. Agustino, dressed in his gray habit, scapular, and cowl (a hooded robe), walked out onto the stage like a stand-up comic. Finding the bright circumference of the spotlight, he settled in and started to speak. Well, he actually didn't speak—he *riffed*. He was more like a jazz musician than a typical preacher.

Within seconds the crowd of young Latinos began to swell—cheering at his stories, laughing at his jokes, and responding effusively to the references and concepts he shared. He spoke with humor, relevance, accessibility, and authority. He connected with them genuinely. The clapping and reactions from the audience were real, not the cringey counterfeit often witnessed when young people respond out of courtesy to a rather lame adult on stage. No, Fr. Agustino *connected* with them. He spoke about things they cared about, in a way that illustrated an understanding of those things—a **shared lived experience**. He had been in their shoes. He had seen what they had seen. He had lived like they had lived. He was one of them. And it was obvious. He moved the whole place.

The crowd of kids—nearly all of whom were Latino and, statistically at least, would have been fluent in Spanish—were nonetheless hearing Fr. Agustino speak in English. Why? Didn't Latinos like Spanish? Wouldn't that be more relatable? Especially in the context of a Latino-focused event? Why did he approach the audience the way that he did?

Fr. Agustino realized that although these kids may have been "capable of speaking Spanish," at the same time, the language of their schooling, their friendships, their jobs, their aspirations, and their dreams was *English*. And yet their **voice**—the way they expressed themselves, their shared experiences, their upbringing, their sense of family and community, their customs and traditions, their humor, and their worldview—was authentically and entirely *Latino*. They were 200 percenters: 100 percent American and 100 percent Latino.

Fr. Agustino Torres, CFR

There are two key principles highlighted by this experience, which I now pass on to you, dear reader. The first is the notion, itself an important insight, that **capability is not the same thing as preference**. Just because I can do something doesn't mean I prefer that thing. And the second is the principle not of translation but of **transcreation**. Let's unpack these a bit.

First, a **capability** to speak in a different language does not, in and of itself, indicate a preference to speak in that language. That may sound super simple and obvious to you, or it may give you a tension headache. Either way, it's true. As an American, you may be able to speak a language aside from English, but whether that language is French, Tagalog, or Swahili, I should not infer that my interaction with you should be in that language simply because you're capable of speaking it! Instead, I should focus on the **context** of our interaction and make decisions accordingly.

But how many times have you been in a conference room at your parish, or in some other ministerial setting, and heard something along the lines of "We need to translate such-and-such because there will be Spanish speakers in the room"? We, too, often don't ask the follow-up question: "Do they prefer Spanish in this particular context?" We generally focus only on capability: "Do they speak Spanish?"

I'm a Spanish speaker, yet that does not mean that Spanish is the best way to communicate with me. In fact, in my case, although I am entirely fluent in Spanish and have lived in various Latin American countries, English would be the most effective language for getting something across to me in the vast majority of contexts.

This doesn't mean that there aren't certain contexts where Spanish would be valuable and advantageous. There are. And in those contexts, you'll find me using Spanish just as much as the next bilingual guy, but the key point is that in the United States, where a question of language is involved, **context matters quite a bit more than capability**.

Now let's have a look at the other principle, which builds on this one: **Transcreation** is the optimized transmission of a concept to a given audience by relying on culture and context rather than literal translation.

Here is an example of transcreation to which we can likely all relate. If I were to share the American idiom "I shot myself in the foot" with a Spanish-only audience, I would not use the literal translation, *Me disparé en el pie*, because people might look down at my feet in horror and call an ambulance! Instead, I'd say the Spanish words for "I inadvertently made things worse for myself." That's an example of transcreation. It's not really about the words. It's about the context and the meaning.

Yet how often in ministry, on our websites, in our parish bulletins, or in various other content messages aimed ostensibly at connecting with our Latino brothers and sisters, do we "check the box"—ensuring the words we wrote in English are faithfully translated to Spanish—rather than focusing on whether or not the meaning we want to convey actually comes across irrespective of the language we choose?

By the way, transcreation doesn't even need to include words. In 2023, the global footwear brand Adidas launched the Superstar Concha, a transcreation of its popular Superstar line of sneakers. A *concha* is a sweet Mexican pastry with a distinct set of markings, similar to a donut, that is often served in Latino neighborhoods, at family gatherings, or after Spanish Masses on Sundays. Any kids growing up in a Mexican-American neighborhood in the United States, whether Mexican or not, or young people in a major urban setting, irrespective of whether they're Latino, would recognize a concha. Adidas, seizing on the insight that **Latino culture and youth culture are increasingly intertwined**, decided to nod to this reality by issuing the specialty shoe model. In the parlance of our times (yes, I'm a big Coen brothers' fan), the shoe *crushed*!

The Superstar Concha was celebrated for its homage to Mexican culture—a design that mimicked the texture and colors (vanilla, chocolate, and strawberry) of the iconic pastry. The advertising campaign to support the shoe featured Mexican hip-hop

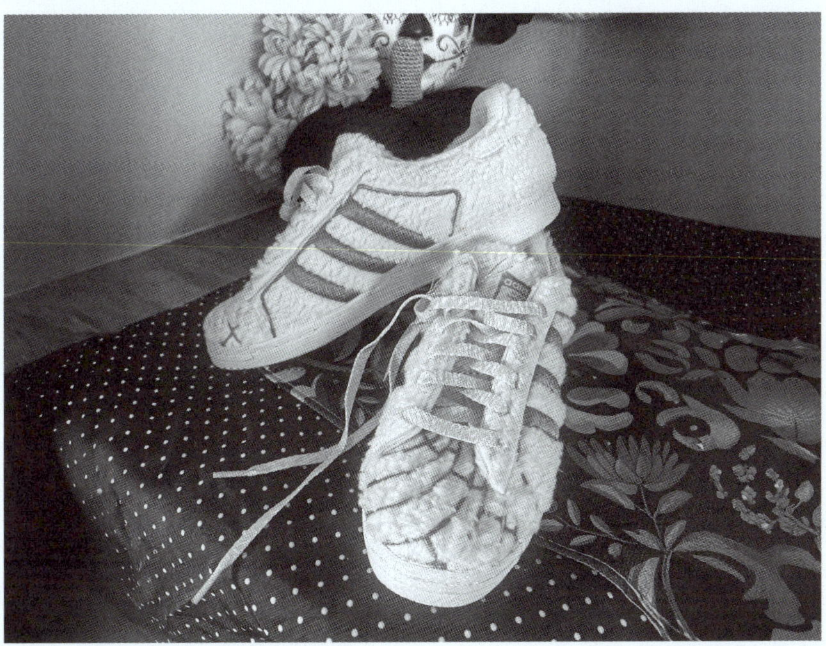

Adidas Superstar Concha

stars, leveraged humor and cultural currency, and resonated deeply with its target audiences.

Memes and social media conversations exploded, reflecting public excitement and engagement. The shoe launch was even shortlisted at the 2024 Cannes Lions International Festival of Creativity, the most prestigious advertising and creativity awards show in the world.

Mattel gave us another example of transcreation a few years earlier when it launched the Día de los Muertos* Barbie. Designed by a US Latino artist, who drew on the folkloric practice in many Latin American countries of face painting and displaying *calaveras* (skulls) during the Day of the Dead celebration each November, this Barbie appealed to collectors and young Latina girls who connected their cultural heritage to an iconic American doll brand.

The success of the doll line went far beyond the Latino community: The Día de los Muertos Barbie contributed to a surge in overall Barbie brand revenue, with Mattel reporting a 50 percent increase in retail-level sales the year of the launch. Subsequent annual releases of the Día de los Muertos Barbie (and now Ken!) have sold out in minutes and garnered price tags as high as five hundred dollars for individual dolls.

Now let's go back and imagine the earlier scenario with Fr. Agustino at that youth conference *had it not been* executed as a transcreation. Let's pretend that the organizers, now suddenly less enlightened, and realizing the event is to be held in Los

* Day of the Dead. If you're Catholic, you know this better as the Solemnity of All Souls, or All Souls' Day, November 2. In Latin America, especially Mexico, All Souls' Day brings with it a series of cultural expressions (face painting, skull decorations, custom-made altars, and other memento mori), all focused on reverencing and praying for deceased ancestors while remembering their earthly lives. As with all Catholic things, certain elements of this celebration have been secularized and co-opted by the popular culture.

Día de los Muertos Barbie

Angeles (an archdiocese with more than four million Catholics, of whom nearly 70 percent are Mexican-American), decided instead of Fr. Agustino to bring in a very talented speaker directly from Mexico. How might that strategy work? Although this person would be a Catholic and speak Spanish, they likely would not understand the context or experiences of growing up as an American young person in Southern California.

Or alternatively, let's suppose the organizers opted to bring in a young and dynamic Anglo speaker from the United States and proceeded to translate her talk into Spanish, projecting it onto the screen in the stadium. The Anglo speaker might be relatable because of her youth, faith, and identity as an American, but she would lack a lived experience of Latino culture.

It's fair to say that the success of either of these approaches—a Latino international speaker or a non-Latino American speaker—would pale in comparison to Fr. Agustino's transcreated presentation. Not because the content would necessarily be inferior but because the authenticity of the **voice** would be lessened, even though the language and other characteristics might be present.

Inculturated approaches always win. And not just in the secular world, with movies, sneakers, and dolls, but in the Catholic Church as well. With souls. Make sense?

Discard Previous Ways of Thinking

- To drive real engagement with Latinos, context and cultural relevance are more important than translations.
- When making decisions about which language to use, think first about your audience's preferences, not their capabilities.
- Inculturation allows us to minister in a relatable and recognized **voice**, making efforts more fruitful and in turn valuable to everyone.

What Next?

- Have I run a brainstorming session with my ministerial team to **transcreate** our latest initiative?
- Have I considered a bicultural speaker or preacher as our next guest speaker or parish mission preacher?
- Have I gone beyond language to focus on storytelling, symbols, devotions, and other cultural experiences?
- Have I built media and content that taps into Latino imagination—music, testimony, family journeys, saints who share their lived experience?
- Have I incorporated Latino feast days, heroes, and aesthetics into the life of my faith community—not only in "Hispanic ministry" and certainly not only during Hispanic Heritage Month?
- Could I encourage my parish to order conchas as the pastry for fellowship after Mass instead of donuts? And not just at the Spanish Mass?

Insight 3

CULTURAL DUALITY IS A SUPERPOWER

Latinos who straddle equally well both Latino and Anglo communities act as bicultural superconductors that drive outsized ministerial impact.

The first time I heard about **code-switching**, I was at a secular marketing conference in Manhattan. As an executive in secular media, I was required to attend trade events in much the same way that a sailor is required to tie knots. As a result, my understanding of the industry was consistently being shaped by gatherings where the latest innovations were breathlessly touted and promoted, whether they were matters of technology or simply terminology. In the marketing industry they are often the latter.

At this point, I'd already heard, learned, and absorbed all kinds of terminology, such as "digital nomad," "social native," "use case," "user story," "cross-platform storytelling," "scrums," "data lakes," and "stand-ups." Certain niche phrases, hybrid terminology, and quirky words would regularly have moments in the sun, circulating in conferences and trade publications like ornate debutantes at a ball only to be quickly absorbed (or not) into the lexicon of the industry. Most of these terms were nothing more than elegant jargon: themselves a species of business-to-business marketing, a way to get people to pay attention to an old concept in a fresh way. Or frankly, in some cases, they were the industry equivalent of clickbait—designed only for the purpose of allowing the speaker to ingratiate himself with the hearer in order to facilitate a quick transaction. As a result, I quickly forgot most of these terms. But code-switching was different. It made sense. And it stuck with me.

Code-switching is the practice of dynamically changing how you speak, behave, or present yourself to better relate in and out of social or cultural contexts. It can involve changing languages, dialects, accents, inflections, or even mannerisms. Most of us have seen this dynamic played out in real life: the teens who slip into Gen Z slang around friends but elevate their speech when speaking to the school principal. The polite mannerisms and careful body posture a married couple might adopt when surrounded by the pomp and regalia of a white-tablecloth gala. Or conversely, the devil-may-care outward veneer a weekend biker might display when pulling his motorcycle into a Harley-Davidson rally. Code-switching stuck with me because I had done it too. I had indeed altered my speaking, inflections, or cadence in certain contexts.

In conversations with my relatives in Colombia, for instance, I would dramatically modulate my American proclivity for efficiency and utility, that cultural curse we Americans have of productizing time into neat chronological use cases like "working lunch," "client dinner," "video conference call," and "stand-up meeting."* Rather than pushing from subject to subject in a mental checklist as I often did back home, I would instead slip into an almost *tropical* cadence—listening casually, taking more time to share an anecdote, pivoting to related subjects without closing the loop on the current one, asking for conclusions or summaries far less frequently, and indulging the repetition of a given line of questioning or dialogue far more patiently.

So, code-switching was a thing I knew. I had done it, and I had seen it done all around me. Some of the anecdotes we've already covered evince this phenomenon. And yes, to some extent all of us, irrespective of our cultural background, do it. But the American bilingual and bicultural Latino code-switches—to borrow a phrase from Tim Burton's *Beetlejuice*—"in stereo." They do it more deeply, distinctly, and more often and usually to great effect. When bicultural Latinos code-switch, they're not just tweaking words to better relate on a topical issue; they're entering an entire new world complete with specific customs, contexts, and cues that when properly navigated can generate great impact and create connectivity between groups.

There may be a number of reasons why this code-switching ability is so concentrated in the bilingual and bicultural Latino, but Occam's razor† would suggest that the answer resides simply in the ability that these folks have, given their command of both languages and cultures, to flow effortlessly between worlds and to authentically engage Spanish-dominant‡ Latinos as much as English-dominant ones . . . not to mention Anglos. And in the ministerial context, I'm convinced that code-switching is the reason why bilingual and bicultural Latinos are effectively superconductors and super-connectors and can act as bridges between

* In the United States, a business conversation "over coffee" typically lasts thirty minutes; in Colombia, you can spend the better part of an afternoon over a cup of joe! A business dinner in the States might last ninety minutes, excluding predinner drinks (itself another type of meeting, roughly forty-five minutes), but in Mexico City a business dinner can feel like a geological epoch, glacial and interminable, because it's packed with every conceivable nicety and courtesy. I remember once having to excuse myself from the table abruptly because my circulation had stopped from so much sitting!

† Attributed to Franciscan friar William of Ockham, Occam's razor is a problem-solving principle that posits that the simplest explanation is usually the best explanation. When faced with multiple explanations for the same phenomenon, the one requiring the fewest assumptions is generally to be favored.

‡ Every person lies somewhere on a graduated scale of ability in a given language. The terms "Spanish-dominant" and "English-dominant" indicate which language a person is principally capable of communicating in. "Spanish-preferred" and "English-preferred" sit between the dominant poles and indicate a tendency to Spanish or English rather than an issue of capability in either.

Latino and Anglo communities in a parish or church community setting. It's almost a superpower.

I was involved with a longitudinal parish study involving thousands of US parishes that measured ministerial participation across everything from serving as lector, to prayer-group attendance, to administrative duties, to church-choir membership. Across almost every category, the most engaged cohort in the parish was bilingual, bicultural Latinos.[1]

Nationwide, this cohort demonstrated an average of 34 percent higher engagement than Spanish-dominant Latinos, 31 percent higher engagement than English-dominant Latinos, and 18 percent higher engagement than the parish population overall. Bilingual Latinos also displayed the greatest level of spiritual engagement when they were *away* from the parish. Whether it was reading scripture at home, visiting faith-related websites, or reading religious books, bilingual and bicultural Latinos were usually more engaged than other Latino groups as well as the general population.

As powerful as this cohort is, it is nonetheless often overlooked in church structures. They're "too Latino" for general administrative or ministerial leadership and "too assimilated" for traditional Hispanic ministries. This perception creates a pastoral vacuum—and risks losing a generation of leaders. But imagine the power of activating disciples like these within your parish or ministerial circumstances, with their statistically greater levels of engagement and enthusiasm and their ability to bridge multiple groups within your faith community!

When empowered, this group can become a multiplier—building bridges, launching ministries, and modeling a new American Catholicism that can be truly transformational and incarnational. Bilingual and bicultural Catholics represent a powerful asset that can be maximized in ministerial settings, particularly with regard to the very real ministerial challenges that exist within the Latino community.

One such challenge I've heard about many times from immigrant parents is the prospect of handing on the Christian faith to their children. Yes, this is a universal challenge not distinct to Latino families, but the immigrant experience presents a unique set of challenges vis-à-vis child-parent relationships. For the immigrant mother or father, communicating with their child requires bridging not only the kid-adult divide but also the foreigner-native divide.

I remember a conversation I once had with an immigrant mom from Honduras who attended one of my talks. She was exasperated by the disconnect in communication with her American-born teenage son. She expressed to me that her son's interests, his questions, his worldview, and his challenges were foreign to her. She could not relate. The fact that her son did not speak Spanish well made matters worse, as much of their communication was limited to the little English the mom possessed and the fading amount of Spanish her son could muster.

In order to successfully pass on the faith to her son, this mother needed to relate to him. And they both needed a way to reconcile their different backgrounds and languages but one that was unified around their shared experience. They needed a bridge, and they are definitely not alone. The need for bridges within and to the Latino community is significant.

In my own parish, under the leadership of our pastor, we've taken intentional steps to recruit, form, and deploy our bicultural and bilingual leaders not only within Latino-specific areas of evangelization and service but, more importantly, within the context of overall parish and community-wide ministries, administrative departments, boards, and councils. By incorporating bilinguals and biculturals as leaders, activators, recruiters, connectors, and conductors in church-wide initiatives, parishes can achieve tremendous evangelical and pastoral impact. What might you and your team achieve for the kingdom with a thoughtful strategy aimed at cultivating advocates like these?

Discard Previous Ways of Thinking

- Bilingual and bicultural Catholics can act as bridges to connect communities—especially when incorporated into general or parish-wide roles or settings.
- Code-switching enables relatability and drives impact across a variety of groups within a faith community.
- Bilingual and bicultural Catholics are generally more engaged, more available, and more willing to participate than other cohorts of Latinos and non-Latinos.

What Next?

- Have I identified the bilingual and bicultural leaders in my community? How might they make a difference in the pastoral, catechetical, educational, liturgical, or operational needs of my faith community that need bridging?
- Have I considered bilingual and bicultural partners (apostolates, agencies, or consultants) that might help me advance my ministerial mission?
- Have I worked to recruit and incorporate Latino voices into diocesan committees, parish councils, school administrations, social media channels, and national media platforms—not as guests, but as hosts?

Insight 4

CULTURAL CATHOLICISM CAN HAMPER GENUINE FAITH

A tendency to conflate customs and traditions with religious observance can result in obstacles to understanding the faith among Latinos.

You've heard a bit of my story already. But what I haven't shared is my journey of reversion to the Catholic faith. Perhaps someday, in a different book setting, I might expand on this testimony, but for the purpose of conveying the following insight, a brief overview should suffice.

As you've already read, my parents were both born and raised in Catholic homes, albeit of different levels of practice, piety, and devotion. When my brother and I were born, naturally they had us baptized and began to raise us as Christians. I can remember early lessons of the faith, songs and prayers that ring the bell of childhood recognition many decades later, and I recall, like flashing images on a screen, the contours of key moments in my sacramental walk: First Communion, Confession, and Confirmation.

In many respects, my childhood evinced the typical milestones of a standard Catholic upbringing—with two notable exceptions that bear on the question of Latino Catholicism and are a helpful backdrop for this insight.

Exception Number One

Being raised in a variety of Latin American nations, all of which could be said to be "Catholic countries," I saw the faith reflected and experienced not only in the worship practices of the people of each nation but also in many aspects of their popular culture. In these countries the line of demarcation between church and state was nowhere near as bright as it is in the United States, meaning that the overlap of the religious with the secular was far greater. This integration of elements of the Catholic faith into everyday public life had clear positive effects, but also some negative downstream ramifications.

In the countries where I spent my childhood, you could find a niche dedicated to a Catholic saint at almost any restaurant. Requests for intercession to the Blessed Virgin Mary were invoked in the most mundane of circumstances and often in conversations with complete strangers. You might see a crucifix hanging in a government agency office. Whole cities were named after martyrs and doctors of the Church. Soccer* players would crouch down to touch the grass upon entering the pitch and immediately proceed to sign themselves with the cross. A telemarketer, failing to close the deal during an unsolicited call, might thank you for your time and invoke a blessing from God on your household at the conclusion of their sales pitch. Pretty much everything—except for churches, of course—was closed on Sundays.

To the more religiously inclined, this might all sound idyllic. But, perhaps counterintuitively, for me this wall-to-wall Catholicism had the knock-on effect of discouraging a deeper, discrete understanding of the faith.

The Church started to blend in with the background. In time, for me, Catholicism became inextricably linked to the other trappings of the culture of the various places to which we were

* In Spanish, *fútbol.* This is a transliteration of the English word *football* and the original, commonsensical, and correct name for the sport otherwise known as "the beautiful game." It's a curious mischance of history that in the American market, and a few others, this prince of sport was somehow tragically christened "soccer."

Sancocho de res, *a Colombian staple*

frequently moving—just another cultural element in a lived experience that included music, food, and people.

The way I saw things, my own personal culture had a series of Latino particulars—a particular kind of food (*arepas* and *sancocho*), a particular kind of music (*cumbia* and *vallenato*), a particular series of social conventions (strong family connectivity and traditions)—and we also had a particular kind of religion (the Catholic Church). Simple.

Once I had equated my religion with any other characteristic of my Colombian culture, it became in effect a kind of **wallpaper**. Visible everywhere, but nowhere really perceived. As I experienced it, the Catholic religion engaged my senses, and in some instances my emotions, but it did not encroach upon my reason or intellect. While God was planting seeds that would sprout later, Catholicism for me at that time remained at the level of nostalgia and sensory experience. And things persisted in that state for many years.

Ironically, it took moving back to the States, where popular culture is most decidedly not imbued with Catholicism, for my faith to slowly begin to move into the foreground. In America, I now had to "raise my hand" in various ways and **self-select** my Christianity for the very first time.

I had to do it on various forms and registrations. In medical records. In college classes that discussed ethics and morality. In political discourse and in any number of exchanges with friends on social issues. Faith, and specifically religion, was no longer presupposed and implicit; depending on the context, it was either affirmed explicitly or politely ignored, but there was no longer any automatic assumption of Catholicism.

Only through a combination of my new American onboarding, years of self-guided inquiry and research, and the occasional debate with a college professor did I begin to discern that my religion, though deeply informed by my upbringing, was in fact something wholly independent of my Latino roots and not contingent on my cultural background, genealogy, or family traditions.

This dynamic is very common among Latinos in the United States. The strength of the connective tissue between Catholicism and Latino culture can often heighten what in effect is merely a cultural observance of the religious experience: a "going through the motions" of belief at a sentimental level without engaging the faith in an integrated fashion. Millions of Latinos, many of them in your own communities, are likely experiencing this same phenomenon right now.

Of course, cultural Catholicism is not unique to the Latino community; many non-Latino Catholics have also gone through the motions of religion simply because their parents or grandparents did so, without developing a deeper, integrated understanding through a relationship with Jesus in the Church. But for Latinos living in the United States, given the unique circumstances we've already covered, the threat of cultural Catholicism is perhaps greatest, and if not addressed, the net effect on the Church at large, given the size of the Latino population, will be most significant.

Exception Number Two

My father was a mystic at heart, a characteristic he handed down in its fullness to my older brother, who today, thanks be to God, walks the contemplative path as a Benedictine monk and priest.

My family recreates traditional cumbia *dress and pageantry at a reunion.*

Dad was a man of great emotional depth, contemplation, and love for life. He was both deeply cerebral and deeply emotive. Equal parts heady and humorous. A thinker and philosopher but with a poet's heart. And he was a great father—a true provider, protector, and friend.

But as my brother and I were growing up, my dad's inclination for mysticism drew him into a number of esoteric preoccupations that were popular at the time. At varying moments in my childhood, Dad was fascinated by New Age or quasi–New Age concepts like the Silva mind control method,* Dianetics, and the "lost continent" of Mu,† to name a few. He read the books, attended the workshops and seminars, and even passed on to us some of the teachings and techniques he discovered.

Unfortunately, my dad's immersion in these subjects coincided with a decreased practice of the Catholic faith in our family's life. We were still Catholic, of course. If someone had asked my parents at that time to identify their faith, they would not have said they were Buddhist or Muslim or in any way denied their Christianity—they would not have said they were "spiritual, not religious," nor would they have considered themselves **agnostic**. We always believed in God, Jesus, and the Church, and we never lost our Christian identity; nonetheless, the ideas and practices of my dad's various systems of philosophical and spiritual exploration were fused to our Christian experience for a time.

So, the reader can conclude that even if my brother and I were not inspired by my father's New Age wanderings, we were certainly *informed* by them. And consequently, both of us, in young

* A Latino, José Silva was a self-taught electronics repairman from Texas who developed a mind-control method in the 1940s. After years of reading psychology, parapsychology, and religion and testing his hypnosis and relaxation techniques on family and friends, Silva launched his method commercially in the 1960s. It originally focused on meditation, visualization, and positive thinking to achieve goals, reduce stress, and develop mental faculties. Today the method is incompatible with Catholic theology—it encourages New Age tenets like harnessing altered states of consciousness, the law of attraction, and even how to "create coincidences to move your life forward."

† In the late nineteenth century, British-American antiquarian Augustus Le Plongeon (1825–1908) claimed Mu was a lost continent in the Atlantic Ocean, equating it with Atlantis. Le Plongeon claimed that Mu's refugees founded ancient civilizations, including the Maya and the Egyptians.

‡ Also known as *ojo turco* (Turkish eye), this is a protective symbol found in Latino culture and often worn in the form of jewelry. It's believed to deflect the harmful effects of the "evil eye," a malevolent glare or stare believed to cause misfortune or harm.

adulthood, did a fair bit of wandering as well. We dabbled in, or loosely held to, a variety of beliefs at different times: Omnism (all faiths are basically the same), Universalism (everyone is saved), even at one point a type of Syncretism that borrowed here and there from various faiths or disciplines to form something entirely custom. A pick-your-own-adventure, bespoke spirituality.

Ultimately, thanks be to God, both my brother and I—and my father—reverted completely to Jesus Christ and the fullness of our childhood faith in the Catholic Church. But this exploration of various forms of belief, and the occasional incorporation of other concepts, lore, and cultural traditions into Christianity, is not something unique to our family but is part of the experience of millions of other Latinos—making it important for all Christians, whether Latino or not, to recognize the reality operating underneath the cultural and spiritual surface of the Latino community.

As an example, there's a young Latina woman I know who is deeply devoted to her Catholic faith and is immersed in a number of fruitful ministries. She attends Mass more than weekly, started a Catholic youth group and Bible study at her parish, consumes Catholic media, follows Catholic influencers on her social feeds, and is in all respects a person of deep and abiding faith. And yet at a recent public function I noticed on her wrist a conspicuous *mal de ojo*[‡] bracelet—an amulet against the "evil eye."

Surprised, I took her aside privately and (lovingly!) asked her why she was wearing it. She responded that it had been given to her by her aunt "for protection." When I explained to her that as Christians we have no need for amulets, and that the Church specifically warns against superstitious practices that place power in objects of any kind, she said she had no idea and quickly removed the bracelet—at the same time adding that she felt guilty about not being able to wear a gift received from her family member.

I share this example only to illustrate the pervasiveness and "stickiness" that often accompanies the incorporation of folklore into the Catholic experience, even among active and faithful Catholics. There are many reasons why this is the case.

Evangelization of Latin America was not purely catechetical but was intertwined with colonial expansion. As we've already seen in the story of St. Juan Diego, for a significant period of time, Indigenous peoples were brought to the faith en masse, sometimes without the benefit of deep Christian formation and catechesis.

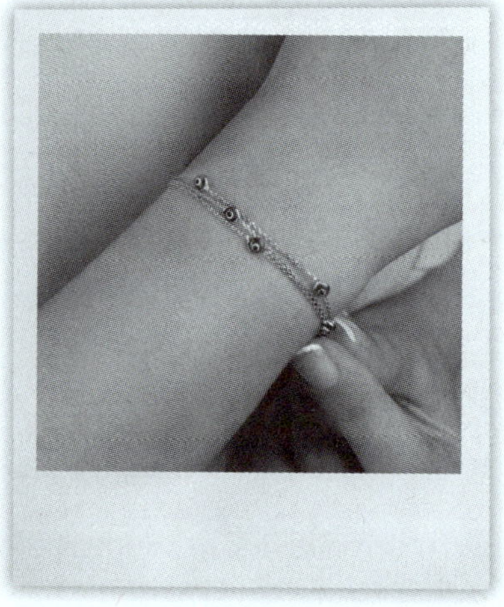

Mal de ojo *amulet in the form of a bracelet*

In this environment, pre-Christian religious symbols, cosmologies, and rituals were often preserved, reinterpreted, or even integrated under a Christian veneer. Family and formation reasons drove the dynamic as well; for Latinos, the faith is often passed down organically through family instruction—a noble and fundamental starting point—but when institutional support for that transmission is lacking, unexamined customs may accompany it.

Combined with the fact that many Latino Catholics in the United States hail from regions where even today access to robust catechesis and sacramental formation is limited, this informal way of passing down the faith has sometimes led to a blending of cultural customs and religious practice, often without theological clarity. The resulting faith practices and beliefs may appear (or even be) syncretic but are almost always the result of pastoral gaps, not willful ignorance or doctrinal rebellion.

None of this, however, should ever be confused with the unique cultural expressions that persist to this day in Latino Catholicism, whether in the United States or abroad. The richness of piety, processions, statuary, *villancicos*,* and physical manifestations of the faith, as well as practices like home altars, *posadas*,† and even *ofrendas* (offerings), may resemble pre-Christian or folk rituals, especially to those unfamiliar with Latino religiosity, but they are perfectly orthodox expressions of Catholic belief and practice.

Discard Previous Ways of Thinking

- Cultural Catholicism can obscure the heart of the Gospel when traditions and customs are valued over and above an integrated Christian experience.
- Latino Catholics possess beautiful expressions of faith—but these must be illuminated by intentional formation that respects their lived experience in order to flourish.
- Blending superstition or folklore with faith isn't conscious rebellion—it's often the result of a pastoral absence.

* The *villancico* developed as a secular musical genre and gained popularity even in the Church in sixteenth-century Spain and its Latino colonies. These were vernacular, rustic songs used to express popular themes. Because the villancico set a precedent for participatory and culturally hybrid sacred music, many Latino Catholic communities inherited a preference for folk-based liturgical music. The legacy lives on today in the United States, with frequent use of guitars, maracas, *cajón*, and other folk instruments as well as songs with informal tone, repetitive choruses, or storytelling structures.

† *Las posadas* is a beautiful Advent tradition involving prayer, singing, and role-playing of the Holy Family going door-to-door looking for shelter for the birth of Christ.

What Next?

- Have I examined whether aspects of my own faith practice are more "culturally Catholic" than an authentic expression of Catholic culture?
- Have I encountered someone in my faith orbit whom I can accompany who may be practicing a faith inherited by tradition but not yet personally claimed?
- Have I been too quick to dismiss certain cultural expressions of Latino Catholicism without understanding their roots?
- Have I considered ways I can strengthen practical and relatable formation and catechetical support for Latino families in my faith community?

Insight 5

TALENT > TIME > TREASURE

In aggregate, Latinos may donate less money, but they give more sacrificially and more often.

One of the most consistent and pernicious beliefs about the Latino Catholic community in the United States is that they do not tithe, or in other ways materially support the Church, as much as the Anglo community does. I say pernicious not because the perception is categorically untrue—but because of how damaging it has been and how much it has contributed to a lack of investment of pastoral time and creativity.

This perspective has resulted in a "brand" of sorts for Catholic Latinos among many pastors, principals, ministry, and apostolate leaders, advancing the notion that a specific focus on Latinos is likely not worth the effort. At our worst moments, even we Christians can succumb to the notion that as it relates to some of our brothers and sisters, "sometimes the juice isn't worth the squeeze." How deeply wrong this is. Let me explain.

First, let me acknowledge that saying pastors and other church leaders have the perception that Latinos don't give is itself a controversial admission. Many don't like sharing their honest perspective on this subject, especially if they themselves are not Latino. Given that my area of ministerial focus is the Latino community, that my professional experience and expertise in the media industry involves the Latino segment of the population, and that my preaching ministry all over the country provides me with access to church leaders, I am well equipped to assure you that this perception is nearly universally held, even if not publicly communicated. But the truth will set us free!

So, is the perception true? Are Latinos just stingier when it comes to the collection basket? Do they not reach into their pockets deeply enough in support of the parish or community? If so, why not? Is it a language thing? ("Latinos speak Spanish, and our stewardship messaging is all in English!") Or is it a technology thing? ("I heard Latinos don't have computers or smartphones or the internet! That's why they don't give.") Or is it a comprehension thing? ("Do they even know what stewardship means?")

Is the perception true? Based on my experience and the studies I've helped conduct, the truth is that Catholic Latinos, as a group across all levels of acculturation and averaging all cohorts, do in fact give less in aggregate dollar amount than non-Latinos. This means that the per-parishioner donation in the United States is generally less for a Latino parishioner than for a non-Latino parishioner. Generally speaking, then, the "headline" that Catholic Latinos overall give less may be technically true, but it's nevertheless not the complete picture.

Averages and generalities may be directionally helpful, but they can also lead us to tilt at windmills if applied universally. In fact, one of the "rules of thumb" that has served me well in my journey to more fully understand the Latino community in the United States is to **de-average**, not average. This means being much more nuanced and thoughtful about what the data actually show. It turns out that the infelicitous headline that Latinos give less in aggregate is not the real story.

Why? Because how Latino Catholics give should also matter to us. And what the data show is that Latinos are more likely than non-Latinos to give as much money as they can every time they go to church, and they are the *least* likely to rarely or never make an offering. In other words, Latinos in aggregate **give a greater share** of the money they have, and they **almost always donate** when they are presented with the opportunity to do so.

This truth reflects the biblical principle of the widow's mite:* The amount of the gift may be smaller, but the generosity conveyed is actually larger. This attitude of sacrificial giving is a hallmark of Latino culture, and any sentiments that wittingly or unwittingly reduce Latino generosity to comparisons between the size of the collection baskets at the English and Spanish Masses run the risk of losing the forest for the trees. The collection basket doesn't tell the full story.

Let me give a recent example of this to make the point clear. A Confirmation coordinator I know recently made an appeal at the four weekend Masses at her parish. Three of the Masses are in English, and one is in Spanish. Unsurprisingly, the Spanish Mass has the highest concentration of the parish's Latino community who regularly attend. This particular coordinator does not speak Spanish, so when the time came for her to make her appeal at the Spanish Mass, she conveyed it in English, and one of the young bilingual leaders in the community **transcreated** her message. More than simply conveying the words in Spanish, the translator made specific mention of both the value of the Confirmation program to the Latino community and their responsibility to support it.

The Confirmation coordinator's overall appeal across all four Masses was ultimately successful, and she raised the budget she had targeted, but the breakdown of the numbers was telling. The three Masses in English contributed roughly half of the total donations, the single Spanish Mass the other half. And while the individual donations from the Spanish Mass were much smaller, they were far more numerous. So, from a dollar-and-cents perspective, the dynamic of giving may have been different, but in the end the Latino community delivered.

* Mark 12:41–44 describes the poor widow who gave two small coins—her entire livelihood—to the Temple treasury, which Jesus praised as a greater sacrifice than the larger donations of the wealthy. The idea is to give from poverty, not from abundance. Proportional giving. Sacrificial generosity.

But since when are we as Christians a people of money anyway? We're supposed to be Easter people! We know the warning of scripture: "The love of money is the root of all evils, and some people in their desire for it have strayed from the faith" (1 Tm 6:10). Yes, of course we need to raise funds in order to support our various efforts and ministries, and in that regard money is necessary. We also need to pay staff, invest in materials and resources—even the book you're reading costs something. But we should neither start nor end our ministerial motivation on the basis of economic impact or return. And no matter how successful the Lord may allow our efforts to be, that truth is always worth remembering.

But why does this dynamic of less aggregate giving exist among US Latinos in the first place? It's clear from data and observation that the lower giving does not reflect a lack of faith, generosity, or commitment but is rather the result of a convergence of cultural, socioeconomic, and ecclesial factors.

First, when considered on the whole, there are dramatically different economic and structural realities that exist for the Latino community in the United States. Let's start with one of the more obvious ones: The Latino community in the United States on aggregate has lower average income and wealth.

Yes, it's true that, like all communities, the US Latino population has its share of affluence. In fact, if the US Latino economy were to be isolated and measured against those of other nations, it would be the fifth-largest economy in the world with $4.1 trillion in GDP in 2024![1] This is a reality that surprises many and has appropriately led the business community to better cater to this important consumer. The Latino community is also among the fastest-growing groups in terms of upward mobility—a phenomenon that has been observed among other minorities in recent American history.* Yet as a group overall, and particularly among more recent immigrants and working-class families, Latinos have more economic constraints.

Included among these constraints are lower median household income, fewer assets, and higher rates of financial insecurity. Many Latinos also operate within a cash economy—especially the undocumented or underbanked. These constraints in aggregate can result in lower electronic giving, automatic tithing, or planned stewardship, which are important mechanisms that many US parishes now rely on for consistent donations.

There are cultural factors too. Latino culture prioritizes giving directly within the family system: Helping a cousin with rent, supporting parents back home, or covering communal costs like *quinceañeras* or funerals are more tangible, pressing, and common means to give than putting a twenty-dollar bill in the collection basket. While these forms of giving are indeed expressions of Christian solidarity, they fall outside of the formal parish tithing structure.

We also need to consider that the concept of stewardship is generally underdeveloped and/or poorly communicated and understood. Rather than stewardship, Latino Catholic spirituality tends to emphasize perseverance in the faith, family unity and support, and pious prayer as core responses to God's grace. Even when stewardship is communicated, it is often reduced to a fundraising appeal rather than being conveyed as a spiritual practice and vocational response. There can even be a suspicion, incorrect as it may be, that stewardship somehow links money to holiness. So, the question of treasure is a nuanced one.

What about the other *t*'s of the classic stewardship model—time and talent? Here is where the story gets very interesting and where the opportunity is greatest.

* Asian Americans have undergone one of the most dramatic socioeconomic ascents in modern American history. Within just a few generations, this group has moved from the realities of labor exploitation and social exclusion to leading the country in metrics like education, income, and professional representation.

Latinos show among the highest desire to bring their personal gifts to bear for the Church and to give more of their lives to do so. They statistically **over-index*** on wanting to give of their time and talents to their faith communities. And yet, counterintuitively, they also show an **under-index** in actually participating in those capacities.

To give an example that might help clarify this point, let's suppose someone is more willing than the average person to go to a party. And let's say that person is also more willing than the average person to bring a dish to that party. Yet imagine that you have data indicating that in practice this person is not actually attending parties as often as their interest and availability would suggest. What would you deduce? One might reasonably conclude that at least one reason why the person is not showing up to parties, despite being more willing to go and more willing to bring a dish, is simply that they're not receiving an invitation! And the

* A marketing term that means a number above a baseline index (average) of 100. If you're a 125 for eating hot dogs, then you have a 25 percent–higher likelihood of eating hot dogs than the average—so you over-index for hot-dog eating. If you're an 86, then you have a 14 percent–lower likelihood than the average of eating hot dogs; in that case, you'd under-index.

† According to the Vatican's *Annuarium Statisticum Ecclesiae* and the United States Conference of Catholic Bishops, there are approximately 17,000 parishes across roughly 200 dioceses in the United States. From a statistical point of view, all of the dioceses (99 percent) have Latinos living within their territorial boundaries.

‡ In the study, *tailoring* was defined in the broadest possible terms. It meant any incorporation of Latino-specific needs into the offering itself. Latino research to determine a new ministry, a service that addressed a particular cultural need, a translated bulletin, or even a profile of a Latino parishioner for the parish's Instagram page could all be examples of tailoring.

data seem to affirm the conclusion that more needs to be done to invite Latinos to the ministerial party.

Returning to the longitudinal study mentioned in chapter 9, and to prove out the point, the average parish[†] in the United States is active collectively in dozens of ministries, services, resources, content creation, and marketing efforts over the course of any given liturgical year to engage and accompany their parishioners (the party). Despite that, more than half of these parishes (51 percent to be exact) do not tailor[‡] any of those ministries, services, or experiences for their Latino congregants (the invitation)!

Discard Previous Ways of Thinking

- Stewardship must be understood beyond dollars; Latinos give sacrificially of their lives, not just their wallets.
- Lack of participation does not reflect a lack of willingness—it often stems from a lack of intentional invitation.
- Cultural stewardship models must reflect family obligations and spiritual generosity—not just financial metrics.

What Next?

- Have I unintentionally conflated stewardship with financial giving, missing out on the time and talent Latino Catholics are ready to offer at higher levels?
- Can I encourage my faith community to convey stewardship in an inculturated way—as a spiritual call, not only a budgetary need?
- Am I inviting Latinos into ministry engagement and participation, or am I waiting for them to volunteer?

- How might I tailor ministry invitations, communications, and roles to acknowledge Latino cultural values and family dynamics in stewardship appeals?
- Can I take a tangible and specific step this month to ensure my Latino brothers and sisters feel personally invited to the ministerial "party"?

Insight 6

COMMUNION SURPASSES COMMUNITY

Parallel paths of ministerial accompaniment, when segregated strictly by language, are a long-term detriment to the Body of Christ.

I know I'm going to get into trouble for this one. But again, the truth will set us free!

When I first discerned my vocation to the diaconate, one of the initial steps I took was to attend with my wife an in-person information day hosted by the Archdiocese of Los Angeles. This diaconate information day would explain, at a very high level, the theological, historical, liturgical, and pastoral role of the deacon, as well as answer questions, provide resources, and make suggestions to the men and their wives who attended. It was a thoughtful and well-crafted experience that further fanned the growing flame in my heart telling me that the Lord was asking me to serve him and his Church by joining the ranks of the Catholic clergy.

But before registering for this information day, I needed to make an interesting and important decision. I had to choose whether I wanted to attend the information day in English or in Spanish. Generally, decisions like these were insignificant; while I usually defaulted to English, nevertheless as a bilingual person I could choose in either direction. But in this case, the decision was *not* an insignificant or rote thing at all. I wasn't tapping the language button in an airplane seat back to watch a movie on a business trip, or attending online traffic school after a speeding ticket. No, I was participating in the first step of what would potentially be a half-decade-long journey of dialogue with the Church to discern if Almighty God was calling me to be set apart from other men and ordained to serve his people for the rest of my life! This was a big deal.

Did I want to start that dialogue with the Church in Spanish? The language of my heart, of my parents and extended family; the language of my childhood, of my nostalgia; the language of the first prayers, sacraments, and lessons of my faith?

Or did I want to have that dialogue begin in English? The language of my formal education and my career, the language of my marriage and my friendships, the language of my artistic expressions and my **internal forum**?*

I recall thinking that there ought to be a different way to design that information day: a way that would not force a decision at the outset to move into a parallel experience but rather create a unified one.† I wanted an approach that would emphasize not only the communal aspects I shared with the other men—the fact that we were all Catholics, Angelenos, male, married—but more importantly the Eucharistic relationship, the **communion**, I shared with them. I desired brotherhood, sacramentality, and mystagogy at the center of my discernment and formation if that was to come.

The initial seed of this idea to better journey with the other men intrigued me, but like so many things in my life up to that point, I left it right where it was until years later when God decided to water the idea and give it growth, resulting in, among other things, the book you're holding in your hands.

Eventually I was received into diaconate formation and soon found that the parallel experience I had witnessed during the information day continued within the formation program itself. I can't recall exactly when it happened, but at some point after being accepted into the program, I was asked to make a decision between an English and a Spanish track for the full five years of formation. Every book, lesson, expert speaker, special guest, homework assignment, practical exercise, and retreat would be *either* in Spanish *or* in English.

In the end, driven by the same reasons that led me to select English for the information day, I once again opted for English. In total, eleven men and their wives chose the English track. Nine men and their wives chose the Spanish track. What would have been obvious to anyone paying attention—I wasn't—was that by making this decision, each of us was incurring a broad set of rather interesting implications.

Twenty men and their wives would spend the next five years meeting in the same place, at the same time, covering the same themes, eating in the same general areas, reaching ordination milestones‡ concurrently. We would clearly be a community. And yet we would scarcely be in communion with one another. Why not? Because while we may have been gathered together in the same building, we spent the day in different rooms. While we covered the same general theological, liturgical, and pastoral themes, we did so under the instruction of different facilitators who employed different teaching methods; we read different

* An "internal forum" is the realm of a person's individual conscience and private decision-making, particularly in matters of the spiritual life and personal conduct. It is distinct from the "external forum," which involves public acts. In a nutshell, when I talk to myself, or to God, I do it in English.

† I'm happy to share that my archdiocese, after consulting with a number of experts, including yours truly, has since created an integrated formation program for all its diaconate candidates.

‡ Within the formation to diaconal ordination (or priestly ordination, for that matter), certain liturgical milestones like the Office of Lector and the Office of Acolyte are formally recognized with a specific Rite of Institution overseen by the local ordinary or a bishop he designates to that end.

books, written by different authors. We heard different testimonies and prayed different prayers.

But most importantly, even though in most cases we were literally only separated by a hallway, we didn't get the benefit of deeply connecting with and accompanying one another because we did not share the moments of spiritual intimacy common to a shared journey. The many births, deaths, pains, and joys that each of us experienced throughout that five-year process were only collectively lived within our different *language* groups.

Does this sound familiar to you? It's a dynamic that is experienced by millions of people every Sunday. We recognize it immediately if we just stop to think about it. This dynamic occurs in

* One of the things I like about Louisiana is that it is the only state in the country that uses the designation *parish* rather than *county* to convey where its citizens live. This approach is rooted in an established truth: A parish is neither a building nor a Catholic community made up of a church and school; it is instead a canonical territory. All people living within the boundaries of that territory are parishioners. Even if they're not Catholic. Even if they're homeless.

† A majority of Spanish-dominant Latinos prefer the Mass in Spanish, and even English-dominant Latinos have a strong affinity to the Spanish Mass. But for English-dominant Latinos in particular, the reason for Spanish Mass affinity is not that they "don't understand English"; it is a preference-based choice (e.g., "It's part of my culture," or "The Spanish Mass is more dynamic and has livelier music and preaching").

‡ This first Mass in what would become the United States was celebrated by Fr. Francisco López de Mendoza Grajales on September 8, 1565. It was conducted to establish the city of St. Augustine in what is now Florida. Some historians cite a number of even earlier possible Masses, but in all those cases the celebrants would also have been Spaniards.

one way or another in every diocese in the United States and in thousands of parishes, and it's this: **one parish, but two churches**.

Every Sunday at thousands of churches across the country, parishioners of the "English Mass" and those of the "Spanish Mass" intersect momentarily in the parking lot—passing by like opposing sports teams at a tournament, nodding or waving to one another politely. Or they overlap briefly in the open fellowship spaces of coffee and donuts, or wait in the same lines to purchase items at church religious stores between liturgies. They may recognize one another, but in reality, they know almost nothing about each other.

And yet all these people live in the same parish.* They work in the same zip codes. Their kids go to the same schools. They go to the same movie theaters and shop at the same supermarkets. They're part of the same **community**. But their **communion**—their spiritual and religious experiences and identities—is strangely limited. They are separated and segregated due in large part to a different liturgical language.

Does this mean that bishops should not allow Mass to be celebrated in Spanish in their dioceses? I told you I was going to get myself into trouble. No! It doesn't necessarily mean that. In fact, the data indicate, almost incontrovertibly, that the Spanish liturgy creates a point of deep spiritual connection to the faith among Latinos—ironically, even for those Latinos who don't speak Spanish.† This is not even to mention that eliminating the Spanish Mass would, in a way, dishonor American history itself, since we know that the very first Mass‡ in what would eventually become the United States of America was celebrated by, you guessed it, a Spanish priest!

No, we don't need to cancel the Spanish Mass. However, we do need to understand, and intelligently discern, the significant **downstream implications** of a pastoral accommodation that is quite young in church years. The offering of Masses in Spanish in the United States began in earnest only sixty years ago during the implementation of the Second Vatican Council as part of the allowance the council fathers made for the vernacular languages to be used at Masses worldwide.

Today roughly one out of three parishes in the United States offers Mass in Spanish, and that percentage has increased fairly significantly in the last decade and will likely continue to do so as the Latino population grows. At the same time, there are thousands of Catholic communities that as of yet have not incorporated Spanish liturgies, and for them in particular, the decision to do so may present a very powerful temptation to "check a box" for Latino accompaniment that, as this book has hopefully made abundantly clear, should be resisted at all costs.

It is crucial, then, for bishops and pastors to reflect deeply on how much they are relying on Spanish liturgies to do the heavy lifting of accompaniment for their Latino flocks. That's a real question. And the answer for each bishop or pastor may yield an uncomfortable realization. But that uncomfortable realization should lead to a creative brainstorm, not a panic!

What might that brainstorm yield? What might come from a meeting to discuss ways of creating integrated experiences rather than segregated ones based on language? In my experience, a brainstorm can yield both big and small ideas. And sometimes the small ideas represent the most impactful solutions.

I recall a meeting I had with my pastor when I first arrived at my new diaconal assignment where we discussed our plans to breathe new life into our parish following the COVID-19 pandemic with an eye to better integrating our Anglo and Latino communities. We planned a series of three parish-wide events to take place in our parish hall, and we met as a parish team to design and execute the events. As we worked on the run of show, we instantly hit upon the need to deliver a program that would resonate with both the Anglo community and the Latino community at the same time. There were a number of proposals made.

One staffer suggested we increase the number of events in the series. We'd have three events in English, and we'd have another three in Spanish on separate evenings (or better yet, perhaps just one condensed Spanish event that we'd somehow persuade every Latino parishioner to attend).* Another staffer proposed we create two distinct programming tracks and have all the parishioners come on the same dates but meet in different locations and experience the programming with different hosts and facilitators.

But in the end, you know what we did? We had only three events. With only three programs. All parishioners were invited. All events were held in the same room, at the same time, with the same program, facilitated by the same host. Three integrated events. And guess what—we had significant representation from both Latinos and Anglos in each of those three events. How'd we pull it off?

We bought inexpensive FM receivers that could deliver audio over a specific frequency, handed them out to any parishioners who *preferred* Spanish, and had one of our bilingual and bicultural leaders translate the proceedings in real time, delivering the translated audio in Spanish over the receiver. And whenever a parishioner wanted to share a testimony, make a comment, or ask a question in Spanish, that same bilingual leader grabbed a microphone and translated to the general audience in English.

We were all together. In the same space. We prayed the same prayers. We learned the same information. We laughed at the same jokes, at the same time. We experienced everything in communion with one another. It was simple, low-tech, and successful.

And it hasn't been the only simple integration tactic we've employed. We've also used Latino culture to inform any parish-wide event programming we've put forth at fairs or fundraisers. Our Grupo Folklórico has frequently performed at parish-sponsored festivities and picnics, and our Guadalupano group has on

* This "better than nothing" approach is prevalent in many places. One implication is that the Latino community often ends up feeling like they're an afterthought. And when they do, they rarely share that sentiment with pastors, clergy, or ministry leaders. But it's there.

numerous occasions hosted the food-and-beverage fellowship after all the Masses, offering authentic *pozole* and tacos instead of simply coffee and donuts!*

But the specific solutions we've employed to drive communion are not really important. You might do the same thing in your faith community, or you might not. You might have entirely different resources, ideas, or needs, and that's actually the whole point! The principle is the important consideration to keep in mind. In a Christian context, communion should always be desired over community.

Discard Previous Ways of Thinking

- Language-based ministry alone risks cultivating separate communities rather than nurturing one Eucharistic communion.
- Integration doesn't require abandoning Spanish liturgies—but it does require intentional design of new shared spiritual experiences.
- Communion is not just about proximity—it's mutual participation in the same mysteries of faith, at the same time, as one Body.

* *Folklórico*, specifically *baile folklórico*, is a vibrant and expressive form of Mexican folk dance that embodies the rich heritage of Mexico. It's a dance form that tells stories, with each dance and its accompanying costumes representing specific regions, historical events, or aspects of local life. *Guadalupano* groups are a very common ministry centered around a deep devotion to Our Lady of Guadalupe.

What Next?

- Have I used technology (apps, AI, even radio transmitters!) to create shared spaces for the people I serve, rather than creating parallel experiences for them?
- Have I defaulted to language as a dividing line, or have I brainstormed ways to use language as a bridge?
- What assumptions have I made about what different cultural groups "want" that may be unintentionally segregating my community?
- How have I actively fostered spiritual intimacy and shared witness across linguistic or cultural lines?
- Have I sought the counsel of bilingual and bicultural leaders to lead the design of experiences that create authentic communion?

Insight 7

DON'T STRESS DIFFERENCES; BUILD ON COMMONALITIES

Latinos come from a variety of nationalities, ethnicities, and economic backgrounds. But engagement strategies do not need to be culturally granular to be effective.

I'm a big fan of *fútbol* (I've earlier made reference to my sentiments regarding the word "soccer"!), and specifically I'm a huge fan of the FIFA World Cup—an experience that arrives for global fans of the sport only once every four years, where the teams representing the top forty-eight (previously thirty-two) countries in the world compete.

This particular tournament is easily the biggest, most widely seen athletic spectacle on earth today—generating an audience nearly twelve times greater than the most-watched NFL Super Bowl on record. In 2022, more than *1.5 billion* people tuned in for the final match in real time, making the World Cup, in point of fact, the most significant sporting event in the history of human civilization.

It is also true that *fútbol* is easily the most popular recreation in the world, a sport played by both preschoolers and senior citizens in hundreds of countries. This is especially true in Latin American nations and cultures where there is no greater diversion. If you're from one of these countries, there's a very good chance you're a fan of the game, but even if you know nothing about the players, the rules, or the rankings, if you're Latino, *fútbol* is part of your cultural DNA.

The World Cup was a rite of passage for me growing up, and each cycle of the tournament aligned with a season of my youth. I was in kindergarten for the first one I can recall, nine for the following one, a teenager at thirteen for the next one, nearly an adult at seventeen for the following, then of legal drinking age at twenty-one the next time one rolled around! Each cycle corresponded not only to a given age but to a time of development. Recall your thoughts and experiences as an eighth grader and contrast them with those of your senior year of high school to understand what I mean. Perhaps this is why World Cup memories are at the same time deeply vivid and wildly distinct!

The World Cup was at one and the same time a personal fandom moment, a family event, a communal gathering, and a religious experience. My zeal was so strong that when I was a kid, I would have given up all my kid possessions, and done any number of chores, for a chance just to stand in the *parking lot* of the stadium outside the least competitive match of the tournament, not to mention actually be in the stands! That would have been unthinkable.

Not only were the tournaments larger than life, but they also seemed to always take place in exotic locations far from any place I could imagine: Germany, Japan, South Korea. It was therefore the realization of a childhood dream, a real bucket-list moment, when in 2010 my wife and I were blessed to travel to Johannesburg, South Africa, for the World Cup final, where Spain beat the mighty Netherlands, 1–0.

What does soccer have to tell us about life? Well, a lot. But that's another book. I bring up the World Cup specifically because as the tournament progresses it reveals another powerful Latino insight, and it's this: **Latinos are varied and diverse, but they will often act as one, especially when the chips are down.**

What do I mean? At the start of the tournament, forty-eight teams from all over the world, having qualified, are divided into twelve groups. (In 2026, for the first time since 1998, the number of teams expanded—from thirty-two to forty-eight.) They begin a month-long bracket-style elimination process, where the weaker teams are gradually eliminated from the competition. In each of the twelve groups, a number of teams from South America and Central America usually qualify—Brazil, Mexico, Costa Rica, Colombia, Chile, Peru, Uruguay, and Ecuador—and from Europe, Spain is a perennial qualifier. In short, if you happen to be a Spanish speaker and a fan of the game, the World Cup gives you a lot to feel good about.

Most every Latin American fan predictably cheers first and foremost for his or her home country. (Although US Latino fans often behave differently.)* But what happens for those fans when their home country team gets eliminated? Do they turn off the TV? Do they stop supporting a team? No. It turns out that rather than become passive bystanders in a sporting competition once their team is gone, Latinos instead transfer their loyalty to the Hispanic team that they like second best! This transfer of loyalty doesn't necessarily mean picking the next Latino team with the highest odds of advancing. Depending on how many Latino teams are still in the tournament, individual selections will vary. And deep rivalries exist between countries, making these decisions nuanced and delicate. A Venezuelan fan, for instance, upon his home team's elimination, would not likely transfer his loyalty to Colombia if other Latino teams remain. A fan of Argentina will not soon pick Brazil. But *which* Latino team is picked after a favorite is eliminated is not really the point. Rather, the point is transferring allegiance to another Latino team to carry the torch.

In the 2022 World Cup, if Ecuador was your home team, upon its elimination you may have transferred your support to Uruguay. When Uruguay got cut, you started cheering for Peru.

* US Latinos will often root simultaneously for the United States (if we actually qualify!) and their home or family country. Free marketing idea for FIFA: limited-release "dual-country jerseys," targeted to US Latinos and sold during the next World Cup!

When Peru was out, you'd be for Spain. When Spain got beat, you'd cheer for Brazil. When Brazil was gone, you were all on board with Argentina. And when Argentina beat France in the final match—**every Latino celebrated!**

Driving this transfer of fandom around a unified Latino choice is the fact that Latin American cultures tend to be **collectivistic**—in contrast with the United States, which is often characterized by a strong **individualistic** orientation. These collectivistic cultural tendencies are caused by a variety of things, from historical structures, to the role of the extended family, to the reality that in societies where institutions and infrastructure are weak or inconsistent, people logically rely more heavily on their social networks for everyday emotional support and economic security.

What this dynamic also illustrates is that the similarities and consistent tendencies in Latino culture are more important for developing engagement strategies than are the many differences that exist among Latino groups. This is actually very good news. It addresses a core question that if left unanswered paralyzes many before they even start attempts at Latino engagement: "Do I need a different approach for Mexican-Americans than I do for folks from Colombia or Puerto Rico or Honduras?" Or the parallel question: "Since most Latinos in the United States are of Mexican descent,* should I just use Mexican culture as my rule for everything?"

The short answer to both is *no*. While these various countries have cultures as unique to themselves as any in the world, for someone looking to develop an approach to accompany and engage the Latino community, the intricacies of Puerto Rican, Honduran, or any other culture need not be mastered in order to succeed.

* According to Pew Research, in 2022, about 61.5 percent of all US Latinos were of Mexican descent, but that percentage has dropped in recent years as other groups have outpaced their growth. The fastest-growing groups are Venezuelans (up 126 percent), Guatemalans (up 49 percent), and Hondurans (up 47 percent).

Focus instead on the collectivistic traits that undergird the Latino experience in general. This is more fruitful for driving the relatability of a strategy, approach, or pastoral initiative across various Latino groups. Principles like the importance of family and community, qualities like spontaneity and attentiveness, and values like interdependence, generosity, solidarity, and sacrifice for the good of the group are consistent threads that can build effective bridges.

Discard Previous Ways of Thinking

- Latino diversity is real, but the cultural common ground is even more powerful and pastorally useful.
- Overcomplicating cultural strategies often paralyzes action—start with shared values, not national distinctions.
- Unity through shared traits like family, faith, and community can drive engagement across Latino subgroups.
- Latino ministry doesn't require cultural mastery—it requires relational intentionality.

What Next?

- Have I delayed Latino outreach because I assumed I needed a "custom" strategy for each national background?
- Am I focusing on common values like family, faith, and community in my outreach—or getting stuck in the weeds of differences?
- Have I invited Latino voices into leadership to help guide me toward unifying approaches rooted in shared culture?
- Could a simple, value-based event, group, or resource begin to reach a wide range of Latinos in my parish?

A CHALLENGE FOR MY LATINO SISTERS AND BROTHERS

In the opening chapter I wrote that while this book is meant for everyone, nevertheless I had a particular audience in mind when I wrote it, that of non-Latinos.

But what if you, my friend reading this book, **are Latino**? Well, for starters, I hope you've gotten value from this book and that perhaps in the experiences and insights I've shared you've picked up a helpful nugget or have had a previously unpursued ministerial opportunity come to you as a result. But beyond that, my Latino brother or sister, is there something special you should be doing now? Yes, and while it's simple, it may not be easy.

You need to prayerfully and faithfully live out your inheritance as a spiritual descendant of Juan Diego. Heed the call to proclaim, preach, and live the Gospel through your unique gifts as a Latino Catholic, use your Latino lived experience to journey with Latinos and non-Latinos, too, and be the tip of the spear of evangelism for the Church in the United States!

This means that it's crucial for you to learn the story of the **sleeping giant** that is the Latino Catholic population and take it to heart. Own it. Communicate it. Advance it. It means knowing the demographic stats of our country and understanding the Latino reality within the Catholic Church in the United States. It means speaking these truths with parish and other community leaders early and often. It means advancing them in the public square and in the digital realm. If not you, then who?

A Latino Catholic friend of mine, a very accomplished marketing and Catholic media professional in his own right, once confided in me that he had purposely avoided discussing his Latino background in US Catholic circles because he thought it might come across as self-serving. But after discovering the data and insights of the Latino community, after learning the full story, he realized that rather than being self-serving, to speak into the Latino opportunity was a way of serving all the People of God and ensuring the future of the entire Church in America. And that goes for you too.

I wrote earlier that Latinos have a higher propensity to give of their time and talents to their faith communities and yet are often not being invited to use those gifts. While that is true, it is also true that we as Latinos should not simply wait to be invited but should also take the initiative to lead—both in Latino contexts and, especially, by stepping forward to lead across the broad spectrum of Catholic life in general contexts.

I recently met a woman who was a leader in the Grupo de Oración* ministry at her parish. Her parish congregation was made up principally of Anglo, Latino, and Asian communities. She was a faithful and pious woman who excitedly communicated all the effort she and the volunteers associated with her ministry undertook each week to organize preachers, coordinate musicians, and join together in fellowship afterward. She also enthusiastically shared the great spiritual fruit that this prayer group had borne within the Latino families of her faith community. And no doubt she was right. I've personally witnessed similar impact from ministries such as these.

After hearing her speak, I congratulated her and thanked God for the group's success. But I also asked her a few questions. The exchange, which I translate below from the Spanish, went something like this:

"Does your parish have other prayer groups?"

"Not that I'm aware of," she answered.

"So, if I go to your parish," I continued, "there is only one ministry where I can engage in the type of praise and worship that your group leads?"

"Yes, I believe so," she replied.

"But what if I don't speak Spanish? Can I join your prayer group?"

She thought about the question for a while. It was clear to me that she'd never considered it. And after sheepish glances at the ceiling, she looked at me and conceded, "No, I don't think so."

"Why not?" I asked.

"Well, I guess it's just for people who speak Spanish."

I continued, "Do you think it would be a good thing if there was a prayer-group ministry that could be attended by all your parishioners?"

"Absolutely," she answered.

"And do you think you and the other leaders could find a way to bring all your gifts into that?"

"Yes, I think so."

"Is there a reason you haven't tried that?"

She thought some more and finally said, "I guess I just never thought about it. And Father never asked me to do it."†

Now, I can't ascribe any ill intentions to this lady, nor would I. I'm sure she had only the good of her brothers and sisters in mind; she simply hadn't recognized the opportunity she had to bring her gifts of praise and worship to her entire parish, not only to the Latino community within it.

* Literally, "Prayer Group." In practice it also indicates a type of praise-and-worship ministry very common in Latino communities, often charismatic in spirituality, that includes music, proclamation, and prayer.

† The Latino population, especially in Catholic contexts, tends to be overly deferential to authority. That means that when a bishop, priest, or deacon makes a request, it carries disproportionate weight. Consequently, however, if the faith leader doesn't explicitly ask for something, that thing is generally not pursued—a kind of cultural "out of sight, out of mind."

This exchange illustrated for me once again the reality that we, as Latinos, need to be much more proactive in general and operate more holistically in the context of the faith community. We need to bring integrated proposals to the forefront; we need to feel comfortable taking the initiative, making suggestions, and building strategies to advance the saving message of Jesus Christ in varied ways to everyone in our faith community. If not us, then who?

So, if you're Latino, your mission, should you choose to accept it, is to carry a piece of the mantle of the responsibility we've been given for evangelization into the fray! Recognize that for the Church to thrive and for the message of the Gospel to take root in our time and place, the Church must mission *to* Latinos, and she must mission *through* Latinos. You are the latter part of that equation.

It's imperative that you prayerfully discern how to offer the fullness of who you are, including the gifts of your Latino lived experience, to the Church for the benefit of every soul in our nation and beyond. This means being intentional toward the Latino community, but it also means being the person in the non-Latino setting—the meeting, the conference, the panel, or the brainstorm session—who ensures that whatever is being discussed will be maximally effective and useful for our Latino brothers and sisters as well.

Epilogue

WHAT NEXT?

My amazing wife of twenty-three years, Jessica, has a childhood friend—the closest of all her confidantes—to whom she regularly gives advice and from whom she often seeks it. This friend, because of a variety of unfortunate situations, had a difficult childhood—one that did not afford her some of the foundational benefits of family, education, and access to economic and social stability that many of us take for granted. But she is nonetheless among the most caring, wise, and attentive people I know. She's also disarmingly direct and has an absurdist sense of humor.

Early in my relationship with this friend, when we'd be discussing topics in the news, about my work, or even in relation to some perspective I might share, she'd often state that because of her background, she wasn't "like me" and that she "didn't know" the things I knew, so she didn't feel comfortable commenting. She said this lovingly, but I could tell she sometimes used this tactic as a verbal foil to distance herself from the risk of saying something incorrect or, occasionally, from even having to know something.

Because this friend is so fun-loving and informal, eventually this tendency of hers became an inside joke between us. Whenever I'd mention some statistic, fact, or teaching that she may not have previously come across, and in an effort to get her to engage, I would end my statement with "Now, you know!" It was my not-so-subtle way of communicating to her that the moment we come into contact with pertinent knowledge about a topic we previously knew nothing about, our ignorance of that topic begins to erode. Even Jesus said as much to his detractors: "If I had not come and spoken to them, they would not have sin; but as it is they have no excuse for their sin" (Jn 15:22). God doesn't hold us responsible for what we don't know. But once we learn something, the responsibility of that knowledge becomes ours. This truism applies to me—as much as it applied to our friend. And, importantly, it applies to you, dear reader, as well.

We've covered a lot. And now you've read it! You've learned:

- There are at least 66 million Latinos in the United States—right now.
- They represent at least 42 percent of all Catholics—right now.
- They are at least 54 percent of all Catholic young people—right now.
- They have massive gifts to bear for the Church—right now.
- They've been entrusted with a mission to bring the Gospel to the Americas—including this America—right now.
- We've only scratched the surface of their evangelical potential.

And guess what? Now you know!

Latino Catholics are not just the mission field—they are a **missional force**. A kerygmatic engine of fire-breathing, earth-changing Holy Spirit potential. If we can start building with them (with us), and through them (through us), we can unleash a new Pentecost in the American Church.

The time is now. Get busy.

NOTES

2. Spiritual Heirs of St. Juan Diego

1. Homily at the Mass for the inauguration of the pontificate, St. Peter's Square, April 24, 2005, www.vatican.va/content/benedict-xvi/en/homilies/2005/documents/hf_ben-xvi_hom_20050424_inizio-pontificato.html, emphasis added.

5. What Makes Latinos Different?

1. 2024 US Latino population sizes from the United States Census Bureau ("National Population by Characteristics: 2020–2024," www.census.gov/data/tables/time-series/demo/popest/2020s-national-detail.html) and Pew Research Center (Jeffrey S. Passel and Jens Manuel Krogstad, "U.S. Unauthorized Immigrant Population Reached a Record 14 Million in 2023," August 21, 2025, www.pewresearch.org/race-and-ethnicity/2025/08/21/u-s-unauthorized-immigrant-population-reached-a-record-14-million-in-2023).

2. Estimates based on annual averages from the US Department of Transportation, *U.S. International Air Passenger and Freight Statistics*, www.transportation.gov/policy/aviation-policy/us-international-air-passenger-and-freight-statistics-report.

Insight 3: Cultural Duality Is a Superpower

1. Unpublished Latino study (Our Sunday Visitor, 2022).

Insight 5: Talent > Time > Treasure

1. *2025 US Latino GDP Report*, produced by the Latino GDP Project in collaboration with the Center for the Study of Latino Health and Culture, University of California, Los Angeles; and the Center for Economic Research and Forecasting, California Lutheran University. Report can be found at latinogdp.us/#.

ILLUSTRATION CREDITS

Images

Page 5, "Dad and Mom at the dance where they first met, March 1960," Deacon Charlie Echeverry.

Page 10, "My family in Mexico, Argentina, Venezuela, US Virgin Islands, and Florida," Deacon Charlie Echeverry, designed by Jessica Echeverry.

Page 13, "*Nuestra Señora de Guadalupe* (Our Lady of Guadalupe)," courtesy of Pixabay.

Page 37, "Facing José Manuel De Urquidi's iPhone camera, Pope Francis speaks on diversity and unity," © José Manuel De Urquidi, used by permission.

Page 59, "Fr. Agustino Torres, CFR," © Fr. Agustino Torres, CFR, used by permission.

Page 61, "Adidas Superstar Concha," Jessica Echeverry, 2025.

Page 63, "Día de los Muertos Barbie," Jessica Echeverry, 2025.

Page 73, "*Sancocho de res*, a Colombian staple," © Getty Images.

Page 75, "My family recreates traditional *cumbia* dress and pageantry at a reunion," Jessica Echeverry.

Page 78, "*Mal de ojo* amulet in the form of a bracelet," designed by Jessica Echeverry, image courtesy of Canva Pro License.

Charts

Page 24, Figure 1, "US Catholic adults by generation and race or ethnicity, 2022–2023," produced using data compiled by *Hispanic/Latino Ministry Media Resources 2024* (United States Conference of Catholic Bishops, 2024), 8, www.usccb.org/resources/hispanic-latino-ministry-media-resources-2024-english.

Page 26, Figure 2, "Religious switching among US Latino adults," reproduced from "Among U.S. Latinos, Catholicism Continues to Decline but Is Still the Largest Faith." Pew Research Center, Washington, D.C. (April 13, 2023), www.pewresearch.org/religion/2023/04/13/among-u-s-latinos-catholicism-continues-to-decline-but-is-still-the-largest-faith.

Page 27, Figure 3, "Religious identification of US Latino adults, 2010–2022," reproduced from "Among U.S. Latinos, Catholicism Continues to Decline but Is Still the Largest Faith." Pew Research Center, Washington, D.C. (April 13, 2023), www.pewresearch.org/religion/2023/04/13/among-u-s-latinos-catholicism-continues-to-decline-but-is-still-the-largest-faith.

Page 31, Figure 4, "Americans identifying as Christian," reproduced from "Modeling the Future of Religion in America." Pew Research Center, Washington, D.C. (September 13, 2022), www.pewresearch.org/religion/2022/09/13/modeling-the-future-of-religion-in-america.

Page 52, Figure 5, "Activities performed on mobile device at least once per week," produced using data from *Always connected: US-based Hispanic consumers dominate mobile, entertainment, and beyond* (PricewaterhouseCoopers, 2016), 6.

DEACON CHARLIE ECHEVERRY is a nationally known preacher, speaker, author, and producer of Catholic film and television. He is the host of *Living the Call*, a podcast about faith and popular culture.

Echeverry is CEO of Black//Brown, a consulting studio that helps major companies drive growth through culture-forward business strategies. Prior to this, he held senior executive leadership roles at global media companies like Walt Disney, Univision, and AOL.

He sits on the boards of John Paul the Great Catholic University, Vagabond Missions, the Catholic Association for Latino Leadership, Guadalupe Radio, Sent Ventures, and SOFESA, a nonprofit that serves homeless and low-income families in Southern California.

Echeverry's work has been featured on EWTN, *The Lila Rose Show*, *America* magazine, *Our Sunday Visitor*, Relevant Radio, Guadalupe Radio, and Catholic Answers, among others.

He lives in Los Angeles, California, with his wife and children.

deaconcharlie.com
Facebook: @charlie.echeverry
X: @DcnCharlie
Instagram: @dcncharlie
LinkedIn: linkedin.com/in/charlieecheverry

Founded in 1865, Ave Maria Press, a ministry of the Congregation of Holy Cross, is a Catholic publishing company that serves the spiritual and formative needs of the Church and its schools, institutions, and ministers; Christian individuals and families; and others seeking spiritual nourishment.